GRIN AND BEAR IT

GRIN and BEAR IT

How to Be Happy No Matter What Reality Throws Your Way

Jenni Pulos

with Laura Morton
and Kathleen King

St. Martin's Press ✹ New York

To anyone who has ever failed . . .

GRIN AND BEAR IT. Copyright © 2014 by Jenni Pulos and Kathleen King. All rights reserved. Printed in the United States of America. For information, address St. Martin's Press, 175 Fifth Avenue, New York, N.Y. 10010.

www.stmartins.com

All photos courtesy of the author unless noted otherwise.

Designed by Patrice Sheridan

LIBRARY OF CONGRESS CATALOGING-IN-PUBLICATION DATA IS AVAILABLE UPON REQUEST.

ISBN 978-1-250-02819-8 (hardcover)
ISBN 978-1-250-02818-1 (e-book)

St. Martin's Press books may be purchased for educational, business, or promotional use. For information on bulk purchases, please contact Macmillan Corporate and Premium Sales Department at 1-800-221-7945, extension 5442, or write specialmarkets@macmillan.com.

First Edition: March 2014

10 9 8 7 6 5 4 3 2 1

Contents

All the adversity I've had in my life,

All my troubles and obstacles have strengthened me,

You may not realize it when it happens, but a kick in the teeth may be the best thing in the world for you.

—WALT DISNEY

Introduction

There are four words my very conservative Greek-American mother thought would *never* come out of my mouth: "I'm dating a doctor."

You see, my always perfect pretty sister is married to a doctor—but enough about her, let's get back to me.

The doctor *I* was dating, Jonathan, was from Chicago and I was living in L.A. On a break from my work on the television show, *Flipping Out,* we decided to meet for a weekend in the Arizona desert. To be fair, Scottsdale isn't really in the middle of Los Angeles and Chicago but it has the nicest weather, so that's the spot we chose for our brief getaway. Our relationship was fairly new but quickly getting serious and he wanted me to meet his brothers for the first time. I was determined to make the all-important, "new girlfriend" good impression. On our first night there, we all went dancing at a club to have some quality "getting to know one another" time.

It *was* all about the music, until a smokin' hot girl approached me and said, "Oh my Gawd, Jenni-girl, I love you on *Flipping Out!*"

Even before *Flipping Out* hit the Bravo airwaves in 2007, I was frequently recognized when I went out, although usually people thought I was Julia Louis-Dreyfus. The look of disappointment on their faces is always the same when I tell them I'm not her. Once *Flipping Out* aired, people began asking me if I was that girl who works for that guy on that real estate show . . . And I'd say "Yes, I combine mints in a tin by flavor, custom order one hundred and forty degree, no foam, nonfat, three plain sugar lattes, and make sure there are ten to twelve red salsas when we have a Mexican lunch. Hi, I'm that girl!" . . . that girl who is now in the position of unlicensed, unqualified therapist to Miss Smokin' Hot in the nightclub:

Girlfriend, let me tell you, I work for a real jerk. I can't tell you his name because he is a super-famous athlete and I don't want to get in trouble for saying too much, but trust me he's a real tool. Do you want to know what he makes me do? He makes me send flowers to his wife, his girlfriend, and his other girlfriend all on the same day! I swear, I am so fired if I mix up those cards. Uh-huh. That's right. So fired. Geez, I can't take it anymore, girl. I really hate my job. I don't know how you do it, working for that guy I see you on TV with every week.

She went on and on about her boss as people so often do when they meet me. I guess they think my relationship with my boss, Jeff Lewis, somehow makes us kindred spirits. So I did what I always do in these situations—I listened. I figured it was better to show her some compassion than to politely explain I was trying to have a romantic night out with my man.

> So, anyway, one night I got a huge bottle of Grey Goose and I was on my bed drinking the whole bottle of Goose. I hated my life so much and just wanted to end it all. But then, I turned on the TV and realized that your life is *way* worse than mine . . . .Do you mind if I get a picture?

I was relieved she didn't kill herself over her professional situation.

"Let's take a picture."

Ironically, the initial idea for this book actually stemmed from a conversation I had with Jeff Lewis. One afternoon, after we had one of our normal everyday visits to dysfunction, he suggested I write a book about coping. At first I thought he was simply being Jeff—the big tease. But then I realized he was right, because I have dealt with demanding bosses, unusual jobs, and sticky situations my entire life where I've had to overcome unimaginable challenges and have *lived* to tell the tales. None of it killed me. In fact, it's made me stronger! When I did things wrong the first hundred times, I learned from it. Now I hope telling my story can be helpful to those in similar siutations.

How would I write a how-to book? I wasn't sure. I really didn't have one specific answer to how I've survived it all. I'd spent a lifetime working for people who have high expectations and who can be difficult. I learned what NOT to do in many of these situations, so this is how I am going to write this book.

THIS IS A HOW NOT TO BOOK
1. How not to look for the "right things" in the wrong places.
2. How not to blame your difficult boss when the problem you need to fix is you.
3. How not to see failure as something to be afraid of.

By the time I was hired to be Jeff's assistant, I was so used to difficult people—they flock to Los Angeles—I didn't think all that much about Jeff's unpredictable temperament. For me, his sometimes confusing behavior felt normal. It didn't seem like it was anything out of the ordinary, at least not at first. Jeff can be a button pusher and believe me, he must have some type of internal radar that knows exactly which buttons to push to get the biggest reaction. It's also who he is and I know it. I can't expect anything different and frankly, never have.

Whenever I meet people, the first thing they ask is how I manage to keep things so cool between Jeff and me. They say things like, "You are very patient"; "I couldn't do it"; "I would go off on him"; "You have the hardest job in America"; "I would have quit by now." A woman even came up to me in a supermarket and said, "When I come home from a hard day's work, I love to watch Jeff beat you up!" If I remember correctly, I believe she said she worked for the Red Cross. Mostly, people want to know what has kept me in this unusual relationship and why I haven't broken from the pressure.

Don't get me wrong, there have been plenty of times over the years I've thought about quitting my job.

Who could blame me?

But I have never been the kind of person to give up on something (or someone) if I truly believe in it.

This is a "don't give up"/"hang in there"/"you can learn to be happy"/"keep going "/"own your own flaws"/"succeed anyway" book. One step in the right direction is to tell the truth about yourself and that's where I'll start!

1

Confessions of a Recovering Me-Aholic

> I'm about to ruin the image and the style that you're used to.
>
> —SHOCK G/HUMPTY HUMP,
> "THE HUMPTY DANCE"

TAKE ONE

Hello, my name is Jenni Pulos—that girl who is the fun-loving bubbly executive assistant, the patient, caring sidekick to Jeff Lewis that you may have seen on television. That girl who has got it together and is always worried about everyone else being okay.

SPOILER ALERT

TAKE TWO

Hello, my name is Jenni Pulos and I am a one-day-at-a-time recovering me-aholic. I have spent most of my life focused on heartache, betrayal, challenges, struggles, and failure. Walking through the world as a self-absorbed, insecure, perpetual victim who never took responsibility for anything that went wrong around me, I spent years feeling sorry for myself. I used to wind myself up about situations and issues that weren't even real.

My MO was to take any situation and spin it into some commotion that was (but more often wasn't) happening to me, without ever taking responsibility. I wasn't the "sympathetic" friend who would lend you her shoulder to cry on so much as that annoying girl you could tell a heart-wrenching story to, and rather than show empathy, my usual response was something like, "If you think that's bad, let me tell you what just happened to me!" Sadly, I would often hurt other people with my insensitivity or be flaky and not come through before they could do any of that to me.

This is my journey of how I went from self-absorbed wannabe to someone who understands how to be happy, and how I went from victim to victor. It was a loooooong process, but one I hope you can appreciate and learn from.

First things first. My self-involvement was off the charts. That was a choice I made and a negative language I readily accepted. There was actually a day when I stood up in my therapist's office and said, "I do *not* need *all* of the attention" before walking out the door because she wasn't focused enough on me. You'd think there would have been a red flag when I called my one-woman show, "All About Me."

Couple that with my constant role-playing as the victim. I played the victim for so long that it became an addiction. Some people drink, others smoke—I felt as if I got something out of that "poor me" perspective. As hard as it is to admit, I liked the feeling of feeling bad, feeling sorry for myself, and wallowing in self-pity. Oddly, I enjoyed it, like having a couple of martinis after work. I became a professional pity-party planner and I was my best and, well, only client.

You could easily say that I had grown so accustomed to being a victim that I could spin any situation on its ear and

Let's get this straight: It's all about me!

make it about me. I accepted all of the negativity because it gave me an excuse for why my life and career were stalled. No motion, no movement, just stuck in the same gear! I remember my grandmother would sometimes look sadly out the window of our beautiful home in Arizona wishing she were back in Greece; she missed her small home and her three hundred sheep. She would make an audible sigh that bordered on a moan, "Oh, the sheep." I'd like to think my negativity has its roots in the Old World but I was looking out every window of my life missing three hundred sheep I'd never owned. Instead of moving forward, proactively pursu-

"Oh, the sheep." Me and my Yia-Yia.

ing the things I wanted and trusting that success would come, I spent all of my time and energy feeling bad about why good things weren't happening for me.

I know.

Pathetic, right?

Like any long-suffering professional victim, of course, I think it all started on the day I was born.

Really.

I was born in Portland, Oregon, on January 3, 1973, to parents who had been trying to have a second baby for more than ten years. My sister, Krisann, twelve years my senior, had made it very clear she did not want to be an only child, and my Yia-Yia (grandmother in Greek) was sure I was an answer to prayers she'd said daily with Krisann. On the day I was born my father entertained the hospital staff telling dirty jokes in the delivery room—or so I've been told. Yes, I was there, but I can't say I remember hearing any of his anecdotes or punch lines. However, it must have had an immediate influence on me because I grew up using humor in the same way. (By the way, my mother has always thought it important that I am aware I was conceived in a Las Vegas hotel with mirrors on the ceiling.)

When I was two, we left the safety of our big, Greek family in Portland and moved to Scottsdale, Arizona. My father wanted to be his own boss, and he was one of the original owners of the Old Spaghetti Factory restaurant chain. He has a larger-than-life personality, and as a kid I remember him playing crazy characters in TV commercials for the restaurants, often dressed as a dancing clam: "I'm Scheky the clam, that's who I am. I am getting ready for my spaghetti." Dad was a hit, and our restaurant was always packed.

Likable and funny as my father was, he was a drinker. When my parents first married Dad's drinking wasn't an issue, but gradually it progressed to become a serious problem. It never reached the point where he drank all day, but by the time five o'clock rolled around he'd pour himself a drink, usually gin or champagne, and then keep his glass full until he got sloppy, slurry, and eventually went to bed or just passed out. Mom referred to my dad as a "Mickey Mantle"

Champagne, Dad, and I.

drunk because he could drink and still function at a high level.

As a kid, I didn't really understand that my father's mood swings were the result of his drinking. I can recall being out for dinner at Benihana celebrating my birthday one year, and Dad suddenly left because he didn't want to "mingle" with the strangers at the hibachi table. What I didn't realize at the time was that he'd had too much to drink. To make up for his abrupt departure, my mom took me to Farrell's for a piggy sundae. (Yeah! The beginnings of a lifetime of *expecting* disappointment served with a side of chocolate sauce and a birthday song sung by a quartet wearing striped vests and straw boater hats!)

When he was sober, Dad was kind, and we had a lot in common, like our mutual love for tennis, a good joke, and socializing. But if he'd been drinking, he could quickly become quite belligerent. He rarely got physical, but he could be verbally abusive. His rage was something no one talked about, even when it occasionally became dangerous. When I was four or five years old, I recall him screaming and hurling a chair across our living room. I hid under the dining room table until the situation calmed. My mom had lived with these episodes for years while family and friends ignored his outbursts because he was very successful and well liked in our community.

At only five feet, mom was a dynamo and we bonded early, thanks in part to Looney Tunes. When I was a toddler,

(From left) The future juvenile delinquent (me), Mom, and my beautiful sister Krisann.

she would put on one of Mel Blanc's records and the voices would come alive in my living room. An accomplished mimic with a great sense of humor (she later told me she had dreamt of being a comedienne), my mom became Bugs Bunny, Elmer Fudd, and the Tasmanian Devil. Often using these whacky Warner Brothers voices, she taught me to work hard for everything I wanted, to treat all people with respect, to be honest, and to—above all—put my faith in God. . . .

She also thought fear and negativity were parenting skills. When it comes to my mom, worry rules the roost. Worry would develop into one of my main addictions, one I still struggle with. It wasn't until much later in life that I discovered worry was easier than work. It certainly was more familiar.

My mom told me that as a kid I was an absolute angel who loved to read and throughout my adolescence wanted to be a doctor—that is, until I turned thirteen. Then, according to her, I became a "teenage terror." I wouldn't listen, I lied all the time, and pretty much became a "juvenile delinquent," as my mom likes to say. Most parents fear the dreaded teenage years, especially if they have a precocious daughter. By the time I hit puberty, I don't think my mom really had the patience for a rebellious teenager. Once I got a taste of what it meant to be social, all I wanted to do was be with my friends. But to Mom there *was* such a thing as having *too* many friends. In her eyes there are close friends, regular everyday friends, and then there are people who say they are friends but turn out to be anything but and break your heart.

"Jennifer, why do you have to be so popular? What are all these friends for?"

"Mom, I can't help that I'm social."

"Oh, yes, you can. You need to pray for less friends. Who needs all the hassle?"

"Mom!"

"And you buy them all gifts on my credit card because you love buying people presents, and that'll put me in the poorhouse. I'll be supporting you for the rest of my life and I'll be dead soon. Then what?"

"Mom you are so out of control . . ."

"I'm serious. I will light a candle and pray that some of these friends go away."

I used my social life as a way to escape my father's drinking. I used to sneak out at night, talk back, and was often totally rude—actually, I was a bitch. I really didn't think I was acting that bad, I mean, really, what teenager does?

When I was in eighth grade, I teamed up with my friends to increase our "cool quotient" by smuggling vodka in to celebrate the closing night of our school's production of the musical Bye Bye Birdie. We were caught and exposed in the middle of rehearsing the song "We Love You Conrad." Hours of tireless pleading in the principal's office by my mom prevented my suspension. What did she say to me? "I am devastated! How could you do this to a little old lady? Your sister was a dream and now I'm stuck with a juvenile delinquent!" My mother's Greek Orthodox faith was really put to the test. She sent me to confession, then prayed to God. I guess he answered her because Bye Bye Birdie became Bye Bye Class Trip to Washington, D.C.

I was a rebel, certainly, but in high school, I found a healthier way to release all my angst and energy: tennis. There was something about smashing that little yellow ball with a racket and daring my opponent to hit it back. I felt like I was connecting and communicating, something I really wasn't doing with my mom and dad. I had a wonderful coach who saw all of my undercover rage and wasn't frightened by it.

"Just keep your eye on the ball," he would say.

I would later discover people make a lot of money prac-

High school senior photo. My smile indicates that I have no idea of the climb ahead.

ticing that exact concept. I played competitively throughout high school, giving me a positive outlet—a way to "change the channel" on my life. I was the chubby chick who could really run around the court. (Greek home cooking sure can pile on the pounds.)

HOW TO CREATE A CHUBBY TEENAGE TENNIS PLAYER

1. Keftedes (fried meatballs)
2. Spanakopita (cheese and butter)
3. Saganaki (flaming cheese and butter)
4. Pastichio (cheese, butter, and noodles)
5. Tiropita (three cheeses and butter)

Celebrating my high school graduation.

I was actually popular in high school, that funny fat chick. I deflected my insecurities about my appearance by relying on humor. I am my father's daughter and I love to make people laugh. I really didn't care if they laughed at me or with me, laughter made me feel safe. Laughter in my house meant everything was okay.

I had a lot of nicknames in high school like Los, poo-poo, or my personal favorite poo-head. I didn't care what the other kids called me, as long as they were talking about me! I was always involved in school assemblies, drama club, and even cheerleading—well, sort of. I was the school mascot, which I thought would be more fun than becoming a cheerleader. I'm not bashing cheerleaders, but for me, wearing our sabercat costume felt more natural than a short skirt and pom-poms. I shared the school mascot duties with a shy kid who was teased for being "girly." When we were at the state basketball championships, someone walked by, punched him in the nuts, and called him a pussy. The only problem was it wasn't the shy kid inside the cat suit, it was me.

"Hey, it's me, Pulos!" I said through the pain.

Later that night, the same group of kids picked me up and threw me in the hoop to celebrate our big win. Imagine me still in costume, stuck in the net, just hanging there. I wasn't embarrassed, I felt popular; they were torturing me but I just *knew* this meant they cared.

In addition to being with my family and friends in Scottsdale, I also enjoyed spending time with my sister, who was living in Los Angeles after graduating from UCLA. Although there is a twelve-year age difference between us, Krisann and I have always been close. I forgave her for being "perfect" and thin because she loved performing as much as I did. To this day, my mother blames my talented sister for "leading me astray." I loved hanging out with her and telling all her friends that I was going to be a big star. I was so desperate to have people see me as being special that I once made up a story that Krisann and I met Ricky Schroeder in the mall and we went to lunch with him. I told everyone he gave me a stack of black rubber bracelets like the ones that Madonna used to wear. I bought the bracelets on Melrose and hoped no one saw me.

This is one of the lame ways I used my creativity to help me deal with my parents' difficult and painful relationship, which no one in my family has ever really recovered from—mostly because we never talked about it. There was so much pain, we didn't know how to feel. My mother, sister, and I had no coping skills and as a result, there was a lot of silence. Very often the only time we'd ever hear my mother was when she was being critical of someone—usually me. My mother wasn't the type of person who would ask if she could give you some advice, she'd just dive right in. Sometimes she was right; other times she was wrong. But always she called things as *she* saw them. So much of what I heard at home made me feel "not good enough." These three very powerful words—the "Big Three," as I started to think of them—became the foundation of the wall I built around myself, a wall I disguised with humor so no one could ever see how fragile and unsure I really was.

They won't hurt me if they're laughing was my motto. As a way of reaching out, I started performing, and it wasn't always pretty. One year a group of friends and I did a lip-synch in high school to the song, "Going Back to Cali . . ." I was wearing a bikini top, which slipped and fell off to one side. I could hear my mother in the audience scream out in horror. That wardrobe malfunction earned me the name, "Silver Dollar" because I had silver dollar-sized nipples. That nickname stuck with me for the rest of my years in school. But it was okay. To this attention junkie, "silver dollar" sounded much better than "big brown areola." They laughed, I laughed with them . . . and I felt accepted.

Looking back, I spent my childhood desperate to get my parents' (and really, anyone's) attention in every way possible. I always needed drama. When I was three, my mom felt my pacifier and I had to go our separate ways. We baked a cake and gathered the whole family to support me with a journey to the Grand Canyon where my blue pacifier would be hurled into its final resting place. A solemn ceremony was created for me to star in. My mother knew the needed good-bye would not take place unless the parting was an over-the-top event with an audience of sobbing family members.

My mom's way to put our household Greek dramas on hold was turning on the television to feel better. I noticed how those funny people on TV could make her laugh—especially Jim Carrey. She looked so happy, even if it was only for a moment. His zaniness spoke to her heart and I could see and feel her spirit lift.

"Please go do this for other people, Jennifer. Make them laugh. Love is so painful," she once said.

I wanted to be that person, the one who makes people happy. In truth, it was my mom I wanted to make smile, because then I might finally hear her say something like *"Jennifer, that was incredible. You are incredible!"*

A girl can dream . . .

On her last show, Oprah said that over the course of

twenty-five years doing interviews the one thing that all of her guests seemed to have in common was a need to be acknowledged—translation, "seen." This is something we all want.

A lot of actors go into performing because they want to be someone, something, or somewhere else. I wanted all three. Many actors would agree that hiding behind a character is the goal; it's easier to become someone else than it is to be who we really are. I wanted to be seen and hide all at the same time. What a mess.

When I was in the fifth grade, I starred in my school play, *The Most Amazing Snowman.* My character's name was, ironically, "Happy." From the time I landed that first role, I genuinely believed that becoming famous would be the answer to my prayers. Little did I know, that if you want the real you to be invisible, become famous. Your various images get the attention and you get to be ordinary in an extraordinary situation.

I'm barely famous and I'm not complaining. There are a lot of fringe benefits, but . . .

TEN THINGS FAME *CAN'T* GIVE YOU:
1. Unconditional love
2. Self-esteem
3. Real friends
4. An accurate mirror
5. Free stuff (You always have to pay)
6. Health

7. Peace of mind
8. Sanity
9. Money (You *can* be famous and poor)
10. One extra second on this planet

2

The Wannabes

From as long as I can remember, I *loved* comedy, and I was obsessed with *Saturday Night Live.* My favorite characters were Chevy Chase's "Land Shark," Bill Murray's "Nick the Lounge Singer," Gilda Radner's "Babwa Wawa," and Eddie Murphy's "Mr. Robinson's Neighborhood." Thanks to them, I started doing solo sketch comedy. The show first aired in the fall of 1975. I was almost four years old. The television had a steady gig as babysitter at Arizona Casa Pulos and I was ready for action every Saturday night. I would go up to the television and kiss Gilda Radner and do my best to copy everything she did. Through the years, I bought every book, read every article, and coveted all things SNL, from T-shirts to coffee mugs. My goal was to be gainfully employed at 30 Rock, and be the *next* Gilda Radner. She managed to make her underdog characters champions and I wanted to learn how to do that.

Following in my big sister's footsteps, I chose UCLA, where I studied theater, film, and television. As a freshman, my days were all about studying, but my nights were spent taking classes at the Groundlings, a legendary L.A. sketch comedy and improvisational theater group. The school has been the foremost comedy training ground in Hollywood and the springboard for countless careers, including Phil Hartman, Cheri Oteri, Laraine Newman, Jon Lovitz, and so many more who would eventually appear on *Saturday Night Live.*

As you know, I had battled my weight in my younger years, always feeling like I wasn't as pretty or as skinny as the other girls. My anxieties were magnified by the beautiful California hotties I was surrounded by every day on campus. I joined the Pi Beta Phi sorority, which only heightened the pressure to be very thin. I went on an extreme weight-loss program consisting of eating nothing but white rice, running four miles a day, and purging whenever I could. I didn't do it all the time, but there were plenty of occasions I found myself with my head in a toilet or pulled over on the side of a road or at a gas station puking my guts out.

Throwing up made me feel like I had some control over my life, which had otherwise been spinning downward for years because of my parents' split, my dad's drinking, and my mother's habit of using criticism as support.

Within a couple of months I dropped to ninety-eight pounds. At five feet, five and a half inches tall I definitely looked anorexic. When I went home to Scottsdale for Thanksgiving, my family immediately noticed my frail appearance. Even though I felt good, I had taken "thin-spiration" way too far. Deep down, I was aware of my eating disorder. But I didn't care. I had gone to California to prove I could make it as a performer. I was terrified that if I ate I wouldn't fit in with the rest of the girls, even if they didn't have aspirations to act. So many girls in my sorority had weight issues that my behavior actually felt normal.

I now know that my eating disorder wasn't just about my feelings regarding my parents' divorce, it was also my insane desire to be famous, no matter the cost. I was so starved for attention that I actually starved myself to get it. I liked people telling me I looked thin—too thin. I felt like I was finally being "seen"; but it was for the wrong reason. I never told anyone about my eating disorder and until now, have never spoken about it. When I sat down to write this book, I realized how damaging my actions really were.

You know what finally changed everything? I fell in love for the very first time with a fair-haired all-American boy; someone I'd dated on and off for six years. Feeling special, loved, attractive, and desired I thought *This is the man I'm going to marry.*

The movie *Braveheart* changed all that. After my boyfriend saw it for the nineteenth and twentieth time, I started getting concerned he was going to change his name to William Wallace, the unlikely hero whose courage and honor changed his country's history. One man making a big difference is, I'm sure, what inspired him to go to Zimbabwe or Uganda to teach. That's when I got a "Dear Jenni" letter from one of those countries that said something about how he needed a princess he could sweep off her feet and I was not that girl.

How many times can you hear "not good enough"? Over the years, I would hear it on a loop: "The Big Three." Let me give you an early example:

You'd think that the experience I had as the mascot back in high school would have been enough to keep me from ever doing it again, but I was determined to keep my mascot dream alive. As a way of showing my true school spirit, I set my sights on becoming UCLA's mighty Bruin Bear. I thought to have any chance, I would have to do something so crazy and outrageous to get their attention they'd have no choice but to award me the coveted bear suit. I had a brilliant idea. When I got in front of the judges, I pretended to pee on our rival, the USC Trojan. Yes, this Bruin Bear wannabe gave an imaginary Tommy Trojan, the revered symbol of USC, a golden shower. Why didn't they select me?

All this time I absolutely believed that I was destined to appear on *Saturday Night Live*. This dream kept me going, and eerie connections to the show were everywhere. I had dated Will Forte in college for a couple of months. (Of course, at the time, I didn't know he would end up on *SNL*!) Not long after

Lambda Chi date party—UCLA with Will Forte. Which one of these people will end up on Saturday Night Live?

KKΓ ΠΒ
MONMOUTH DUO 19

Will and I broke up, I was fixed up on a date with a guy who told me his brother was going to be on *SNL* while we were riding a Ferris wheel.

"I'm going to be on *SNL*, too!" I blurted out, totally believing it.

A few weeks later, his brother made his official *SNL* debut. It was Will Ferrell. Seeing him on the show and recognizing his immense talent motivated me more than ever. His comedy fearlessly flew without a net in skits like "Dissing Your Dog Pet Training Video," "Janet Reno's Dance Party with her D.O.J. (Dances of Janet)," and the unforgettable "Spartan Cheerleaders of East Lake High" who cheered on the ping-pong and chess teams. I was going to find a way to someday share the stage at the infamous NBC Studio 8H.

Around my junior year, I thought that I'd spent enough time working my way up at the Groundlings and it was finally my chance to be a part of the troupe.

To become one of the thirty official members, you had to audition. My hopes were high of joining this company whose members write and perform in their theater shows and teach classes at the school. One of the instructors there decided to crush my dream. For the audition, I had created a character called Carol Pitts. She was a talkative, nerdy office worker whose life revolved around sex and syntax errors. She would have imaginary orgasms with her imaginary boyfriend in her very real office cubicle panting, "I love him. I hate him. I love him. I hate him." It didn't go over well.

"Lorne Michaels would love you because you have big tits and a high squeaky voice, but you're not funny!" the teacher said after I finished my scene.

Ouch.

Maybe she didn't like other funny women?

Surely she didn't really mean what she was saying.

How could she?

Chris Kattan, who was already in the company, leaned over and whispered, "Hang in there . . . " as I slouched my entire body until I looked like a small hedgehog and scurried back to my seat. Truth be told, I was mad. I thought I was funny. If you are going to tell me I'm not funny, at least give me some solid reasons why you feel that way. There was nothing constructive about her telling me how she really felt, except, perhaps . . . could it be, she was telling me the *truth*? I sat there for the rest of the performances, spinning her reaction over and over in my head. Why was I attracting such a negative response from this person?

At first I just thought, *She's an angry, jealous woman who was taking her own frustrations out on me.* Ultimately I spent way too much time analyzing why she didn't like me instead of being willing to learn what I could have done to improve my performance. I recently came across her critique sheet, and looking at it today, she was absolutely right and spot-on with her insight. I certainly could have worked harder on the scene and developed the character more so the audience cared about her. But I didn't even care about her! That was the problem! What I did care about was what other people thought of me. I was just seeking validation, which of course I didn't get. I certainly wasn't getting the validation I was seeking from comedy, either. So I decided to shift my focus and prove that I could do something else, dramatic acting. I know . . . I'll try out for Shakespeare! That will show everyone how talented and versatile I am!

Shakespeare classes!

England's national poet became my main man. By the time I was in my senior year, I was the only person from UCLA to get not one but two of the lead roles in the all-women's production of Shakespeare's, *Macbeth.* I was cast as Malcolm and McDuff. I worked harder on that audition than I had ever worked on anything, and everyone was completely blown

I was told this big chair would make me look perfect for a sitcom. (Photo Credit: Lori Dorn)

away. R-E-S-P-E-C-T. That's what Shakespeare meant to me. No one expected me to audition for the roles, let alone get them. I must confess I enjoyed giving my critics the classical finger. But once I got the roles, I didn't work as hard as I did in preparing my audition. As a result, I wasn't able to deliver my best performance show after show. Looking back, I can now see that it wasn't about my desire to actually act—it was all about being validated. It wasn't about the work or the journey. It was about the destination—to be SEEN.

Unfortunately, most of my teachers at UCLA still saw me as a lifelong waitress in training. I was dumped in the it's-never-gonna-happen heap, because my voice was annoying and I was too one-dimensional. Many years later, I read that Carol Burnett's teachers told her something similar. That may be the only thing we have in common, but if her success was any indication of what was possible, there's always hope!

> I have always grown from my problems and challenges when things don't work out. That is when I've really learned.
>
> —CAROL BURNETT

After graduating, I did what a lot of struggling actors do—I tried to follow in the footsteps of the already famous. Pre-fame Michelle Pfeiffer worked as a bagger at Vons Supermarket and if she could do it, so could I! I visibly cringed when one of my former teachers from UCLA came into the grocery store I was working at in Beverly Hills and, of course, through my checkout line. When she recognized me she effortlessly avoided me and said under her breath, "Of course *you're* here," as she walked away.

It was awful. I spent my break crying my eyes out in the employee bathroom. I later blamed my puffy red eyes on "pesky allergies." (Lying seemed to be always coming to my rescue.)

It was right around this time that I met my first husband, Chris Elwood. We were both struggling actors and had been set up on a blind date by our managers. They were two handsome, charming guys who wore really nice Armani suits, drank expensive champagne, and smoked fancy Cuban cigars.

Chris and I celebrating our engagement with a glamour shot at Super Walmart.

Oddly, they never talked about work. I had no idea how to talk about my career in a serious way, so why would they? We partied and obsessed about what was in the tabloids. Celebrity was the name of the game! I knew they were going to parent me and my career into the winner's circle. "Jenni, you are going to be a huge star!" I was having ear-gasms and not noticing that my career was headed into oblivion. And of course they knew the perfect partner for me! My life and career were in great hands. What was I thinking? I wasn't.

Chris was a handsome, gifted actor and comedian who I immediately found extremely attractive. His Jim Carrey impersonation was spot-on! This was the man I could bring home to Mother! We started performing with each other, doing improvisational work, independent films, and even wrote together. Before we knew what hit us, we were "in love."

Two years into our relationship, I was ready to get married. Although my parents divorced, I grew up believing in the sanctity of marriage and strong partnerships; I think commitment and the sacrament itself are important. Chris had been married once before to another girl named Jenny—with a *y*. He told me the Jenny-with-a-y relationship hadn't ended well. When we met, Chris was still living with his ex-wife, which he failed to tell me until our fourth date. I promptly dumped him and, of course, three minutes later I took him back. Chris sort of asked me to marry him during a flight we were on from LA to New York.

"So, you wanna do this or what?" It wasn't exactly the romantic proposal I'd always dreamt of, but at the time, it was good enough for me. Besides, I thought I loved Chris and very much wanted to marry him. So of course, I said yes.

We were flat broke. Which meant I had to buy my own engagement ring. Paying for my engagement ring was a red flag I chose to ignore.

RED FLAGS THAT TELL YOU
THE PRINCE PROBABLY ISN'T CHARMING

1. He can't stop talking about his ex (wife or girlfriend).
2. He doesn't like his mother.

3. He is too attached to his mother.
4. He wants you to be his mother.
5. He has bad credit.
6. He wants to move in right away to your apartment (house, etc.).
7. He writes sexy e-mails…but not to you.
8. He knows your family is rich and that's a big plus.
9. He knows your family is poor and that's a big minus.
10. He avoids maturing because he thinks it will interfere with his creativity.

So, I purchased the ring on my credit card and my mom was going to pay for our big fat Greek wedding.

After Chris and I were engaged, I wrote and produced my first one-woman show titled, *All About Me* ... It was eight characters in search of sanity. The nowhere-near-ready-for-primetime players included a former child star in rehab, her stage mom, her dialect coach, and a lounge singer named Wendy Saperstein. One evening, midsong, Wendy encountered a heckler, so she sat on him and rubbed his head. To my surprise, it became one of the best parts of the show.

All About Me ran for a couple of months, sold out every night, and actually got pretty good reviews. It was selected as a top comedy pick by *LA Weekly*. On closing night, a talent scout from *Saturday Night Live* was supposed to come see me. But lucky me, a banana truck flipped over on the 405 freeway, snarling traffic for hours, so he never made it. The result:

STILL NOT SEEN. My dream of being on *SNL* was dashed by a bunch of bananas!

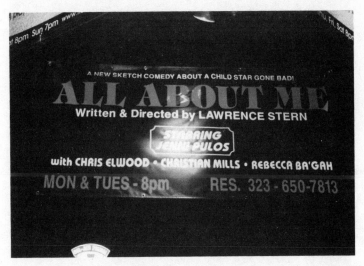

My one-woman show—2000.

After my one-woman show closed, Chris and I were married in Palm Desert where my mom and sister lived. Afterward, we immediately left for our honeymoon in Greece. We were both in our mid-twenties and thought we were as happy as could be. Sometime during that trip Chris told me he cried at his first wedding because he knew it wasn't right. But he said he didn't cry at our wedding because this time he was certain he married the right girl.

Shortly after our honeymoon, Chris's career really started taking off, and to be completely honest I was jealous. *I* wanted to be the successful one. He tried to reassure me and build up my confidence by saying I was the truly unique personality in our family, but somehow that didn't make me feel any better. *Unique* is the kind of word used in show business when they think your talent is not marketable and you're just not pretty enough. I was pretty alright, as in pretty much the "funny" friend or the token fat chick. They were the only roles I was auditioning for and I often wasn't even getting *those* parts. At the time, every headshot I had made me look scared, petrified, and chubby. Which makes sense, because I *was* scared, petrified, and chubby.

Once in a while I did get a minor part. My small role in the movie *The Bachelor* paid for my breast reduction. Most girls in L.A. pay to get them enlarged and I, of course, went in the other direction.

Chris O'Donnell's reaction when I told him, "This job is paying for my breast reduction."

When I wasn't working odd jobs, I spent my time at Hollywood premiers, B-list celebrity-studded parties, and industry events so I could feel as if I belonged—even if I was on the outside looking in. I got so excited when I saw a picture of my shoe in one of the magazines next to a celebrity, I actually ran around showing everyone the magazine, "Hey! That's my shoe!"

I was okay with being a sidekick for a while—the invisible girl who stands off to the side holding someone else's coat and handbag as they walked the red carpet, "believing" what everyone was telling me, that I wasn't pretty enough or talented enough to someday walk it myself. After all, I kept hearing "no, no, no, this is your line *behind* the curtain, *this* one is for talent, only!"

Finally it all just got tired: that layer of excess fat that I wore as a protective coat; that kooky exterior I hid behind; the sadness I felt getting pushed aside for someone who seemed to be better. I wanted to be sexy, stunning, sophisticated, and special—all words that begin with an "S" I never thought I'd hear people say about me. Hey, if you're going to dream, dream big.

I wanted to start at the top! So Chris and I started to develop scripts that involved characters we had performed at local comedy clubs. These characters had repeatedly survived hearing the audience react with such things as "Get off the stage," "You suck," and lots of other stuff my mother would not like to see in print. One of my characters was Gordy, a short man with a receding hairline who had a passion for clog dancing. Chris played Lolly, a vain, self-obsessed, wan-nabe actress I'm sure he based on me. We wrote a love story that could work as either a feature film or a television series. Gordy was desperate to become a champion clog dancer, and had reconnected with the love of his life, Lolly, at the finals of an international clog dancing competition. Lolly came from a rich family who didn't want her to be with Gordy because they didn't think he was good enough for her. After break-ing up, to spite her parents, Lolly quickly marries the origi-nal *Super Freak* and habitual line-stepper, Rick James. I'm serious.

One afternoon, we were driving back from a Gordy and Lolly appearance at Luna Park, a restaurant on Melrose. We were both still in our costumes when we got into a huge fight. I told Chris to get out of the car. I dropped him on La Cienega, a very busy street in West Hollywood. Seeing a man dressed in drag isn't necessarily a strange sight in West Hollywood, but it always makes me laugh thinking of Chris stranded on the street dressed as Lolly as I sped off as Gordy. (The fact is that Gordy and Lolly probably got along much better than we did!)

In 2004, while trying to get people interested in the Gordy and Lolly script, we developed a pilot presentation with a friend who very much believed in the project—enough that he put up his own money for all of the production costs. We started shooting in the fall of 2005.

I had an orthodontist friend of mine make a set of braces for Gordy to wear to add to his goofy, nerdy look for a flashback scene of him in high school. My friend sent them via overnight courier several days in advance of the shoot, but they never arrived. On the day we were set to film, I called the delivery company to see if they could help me track the missing package. They said they couldn't. If I wanted to search for the box, I would have to drive to their main facility an hour south from where we were shooting. I was determined to wear those braces so I got into my car dressed as Gordy and that little man drove like a bat out of hell. When I arrived, the clerk behind the desk told Gordy that it was against their company policy to let anyone not employed there in the warehouse or on the trucks.

"You don't understand!" I pleaded with the clerk. "I'm a woman playing a man for a movie and he wears braces. If I don't get that box, my life will be *over!*"

The clerk looked at me with a blank stare.

"Do you have a dream?" I asked, sincerely but perhaps a bit overly dramatic. "Do you understand how important it is to follow your dreams? If you don't let me get on that truck and get Gordy's braces my life will be ruined!" I offered my driver's license and credit card as two forms of identification to prove I wasn't a total freak, which worked. Realizing this little man with a mustache, receding hairline, and stuffed socks in his pants wasn't leaving without that box, the clerk even helped me find the package. I wasn't willing to take no for an answer. This time determination and perseverance really paid off.

Gordy—a man I could always count on.

Even though we had interest in the Gordy and Lolly script from the Farrelly Brothers (*Dumb and Dumber, There's Something About Mary*), we couldn't seem to get anything off the ground. Luckily, it sparked another idea for a reality show called, *The Wannabes*. Reality television was still in its infancy back in 2006. I'm not sure anyone really expected it to take over scripted shows the way that it did, but I really believed in every ounce of my being that we were onto something. We wanted to create a show that could have been a child of *Curb Your Enthusiasm*. Like *Curb*, it was supposed to

Rehearsing for Showtime
at the Apollo—*2002*.

be semiscripted but would follow our actual lives. The plot was based on us (of course!), trying to make it in Hollywood as actors and, in my case, as a rapper, too.

Holla!

My rapping career was actually born back at UCLA when I was in a comedy rap group called Juicy. Nothing was off limits. We even turned the funky fresh jam "Supersonic" by J. J. Fad into a remix called "Liposuction." Then, in 2002, I entered the infamous *Showtime at the Apollo* talent show as a rap duo with Todd Lewis, Jeff's brother. But more on my TV better half later.

If you aren't familiar with *Showtime at the Apollo,* the crowds are notoriously rough. They will boo anyone off the stage with such vigor, it's often terrifying to even think about going out there. If you can survive amateur night at the Apollo, you can survive anything. That audience is known as one of the toughest in the business. Knowing this, Todd and I decided to go for it. I haven't always known where I'm going in life, but like most hard-core rappers, here is where I have to give thanks to God.

We were the second to last act that night, following a Japanese dance team, Aretha Franklin's doppelgänger, Barry White's doppelgänger (with a bigger tongue), a Boyz II Men a cappella–style group with three of the most beautiful African American men I have ever seen, and a hot sexy singer who came out and killed it with her voice and body, not in that order. The crowd had gone crazy for each one of these performers. And then it was our turn.

I didn't know if the producers were setting us up for a fall by putting us toward the end of the show or if they knew it would be great television to have two extremely white nerdy rappers go out on that great big brutal stage. Just before Todd and I went on, Kiki Shepard and Rudy Rush, the co-hosts of the show, were looking us up and down, like we'd stumbled into the wrong hood. All I could think was, *Don't forget to rub the stump.* There's a tradition to rub what remains of the tree of hope, a lucky wishing tree that was cut down in 1934. A legendary section of the trunk sits at the side of the stage.

Rubbing the stump is known to bring good luck and has been a longstanding tradition for amateur night for many years.

Chris and Todd's girlfriend, Carrie, were in the audience. You could easily spot them in the crowd. Chris was standing next to an Apollo regular who asked why he was there.

"My wife is performing tonight."

"Aw, great, man, I'll cheer for her . . . ."

When the Aretha Franklin look-alike came out he turned to Chris and asked, "Is that your wife?'

"No."

When the Japanese dance team came out, he turned and asked, "Is that your wife?"

"Nope."

When the hot sexy African American girl came out, he asked, "Is *that* your wife?"

"Nuh-uh."

Finally, when I came out, he turned to Chris and said, "Oh no, man, please tell me that's not your wife . . . ."

"Uh, yeah . . . that's my wife . . . ."

"I can't do it, man . . . sorry . . . ."

The minute we stepped onto the stage—me in a Brownie uniform, beanie and all, and Todd in Boy Scout shorts, thick black glasses, and a green sash full of Cub Scout badges across his chest—we were booed and laughed at. The host Rudi Rush introduced us.

"I'm Jenni, yeah."

"I'm Todd."

"And we're from Los Angeles."

I announced meekly that we were going to do "a little song from camp . . . God Bless New York." We wanted to be SEEN. And boy, were we ever.

As expected, the crowd was raucous and had no time for our brand of silliness. People were visibly cringing in their seats, holding their hands over their open mouths in horror. The music started and we began our ultra-white, super-geeky dance moves, complete with lip biting and protruding thumbs. But as soon as the music kicked in and turned into a beat, we quickly transformed into street badasses attacking with the words, "Who's the black sheep? What's the black sheep? Here they come, yo, here they come."

We covered the stage with our moves repeating, "You can get with this. And you can get with that." We stunned the crowd, including the Apollo regular next to Chris. Everyone was on their feet, clapping, fist pumping, whoop-whooping it up and having a great time. When we finished, one of the hosts came back to congratulate me.

"Girl, come here and give Kiki a hug!" she said as she threw her arms around me.

To announce the winner of the show, the producers bring each of the acts back on stage for a final audience vote. Todd and I stood up there with all of this amazing talent waiting to hear who won. When they announced that we had tied for first place, the crowd went nuts—but then, they were asked to break the tie and scream for the winner and we lost to the a capella group. But it was an incredible moment. For the first time in my career I felt SEEN. Finally I'd done something I thought would make my mother proud—and happy. I wanted to keep my big win a surprise, so I didn't tell her the results of the show that night. I simply told my mom when the show was set to air, and warned her that since the show came on so late at night, she had to promise to stay awake for the entire episode or she would miss the big surprise at the end. I knew she'd call me the next morning.

When the phone rang early the next day, I was sure I was about to get my mother's approval—it was a moment I'd been waiting for my entire life. "Jennifer, I saw your show," she said. Here it comes . . . the moment I had been waiting for.

"Did you like it Mom?"

"It was horrible," she said.

My heart sank. I knew full well she wouldn't approve of me rapping, dressed as a Brownie, gyrating my pelvis in front of three thousand strangers, but I held out hope that she might somehow come around. I asked her why she didn't like the show.

"Well, that man was on the whole time selling that cheap face cream, which looks like a terrible product. I guess you came out toward the end of the two-hour segment, but Jennifer, it didn't even look like you. Did you straighten your hair and gain weight since the last time you came to Palm Springs? Your ankles looked less swollen, though, so that was good."

That ankle comment was my mom's way of being supportive. I tried not to react.

"Mom, what channel were you watching?"

"Oh, I don't remember. I think the peacock," she said.

"Didn't you check *TV Guide*? The show was probably preempted and replaced by infomercials because I wasn't selling face cream. I was a rapping Brownie!"

"Oh, Jennifer just get in something I can be proud of already! Nia Vardalos's mom gets *My Big Fat Greek Wedding* and I'm stuck with a rapping Brownie."

You have to love my mother's version of nurturing.

With her approval ever-present in my mind, I actually thought *The Wannabes* might be something that would make my mom happy. As a way of hedging my bet, I put her in *The Wannabes* pilot. She did some great improvising, including my always asking her for money. To be fair, there wasn't a lot of imagination needed as I was still asking my mom for money all the time—in fact, she called us the "Needabees." Still, she helped make those exchanges feel just a little funnier and more authentic because of her no-holds-barred candor.

The original concept for *The Wannabes* was about Chris and I doing odd jobs as we struggled for that big break. Enter Jeff Lewis. Jeff was a professional house flipper and real estate developer in Los Angeles, and he had hired Chris to be his house assistant long before we came up with the concept for our show. Then one day, I filled in for Chris because, naturally, he had an audition and I didn't. Whenever Jeff spoke throughout the day, I took detailed notes so I wouldn't forget to do anything he wanted me to do. Little did I know that perfectly executing the delivery of a honey-glazed ham would end up in a job offer: He wanted one for his grandmother, and he was over-the-moon thrilled when the ham had been delivered exactly to his specifications. I sealed the deal with a Post-it listing of who he needed to call over the weekend. He immediately offered me a job as his executive assistant, and I agreed to work for him on the condition that he would let me go on auditions whenever I needed to.

Up until then, I had been waiting tables around L.A. and doing odd jobs, and I was completely over that lifestyle. A secure job with a steady paycheck would be a new experience. Besides, I thought, when I make my money acting, I'd like to know more about real estate because it could be a smart investment.

Initially, Jeff was only supposed to have a small role—and even that was a tough sell to him. Convinced I needed him for authenticity and a little drama, I pleaded with Jeff to participate. Despite his consistent refusal, I gave it everything I had to wear him down and get him to say yes. Whenever we were driving around I would slip into our conversations:

"You will earn extra money."

"You'll be able to showcase your skills."

And I promised, "it wouldn't take much of your time." I was literally still begging the day before the shoot and he was still saying "no."

As I talked, Jeff became so distracted with his handyman washing his filthy outfit in a client's brand-new washer and dryer that he finally surrendered. Chris and I celebrated. We were well on our way to becoming famous.

Jeff loved buying homes, fixing them up, and selling them for a tidy profit. At that time, Jeff had flipped about fifty or so homes. In 2007, the real estate market hadn't dropped out yet and the economy was still on the up and up, so Jeff was on a real roll. He didn't need the show, nor did he really share my dream of being famous. However, after much shameless begging, he finally, albeit unhappily, agreed to do it—for me. Good thing, too, because his "yes" came on the night before our first day of filming our sizzle reel, an edited overview of what the show would look like. It's like a movie trailer, designed to interest the networks and get them to pick up the idea and fund a pilot or series.

Jeff was amazing and hilarious in the sizzle reel and was as unfiltered then as he is today. Jeff had agreed to do the reel as a favor and wasn't the least bit interested in seeing this concept go any further, but he proved to have a charm that was really appealing. Although he was not the focus of the show, he was "a natural," comfortable being truthful about who he is, which is why people loved what they saw when they got a glimpse of Jeff on-screen. We thought for sure we had a good chance at selling our show.

By the time we shopped *The Wannabes,* Hollywood "inside" shows weren't working anymore, including the ones with big stars—*Kilroy*, a pilot George Clooney produced, and *The Comeback* with Lisa Kudrow had been canceled. And as it turned out, Jeff was apparently very attractive to the network executives—more than we were. Why? He was charming, handsome, *and* successful.

I couldn't even win selling myself as a loser!

The more people saw our sizzle reel, the stronger they came back saying they loved Jeff's fiery personality. Jeff's business was in high gear and he didn't care whatsoever about having a show, which only enhanced his credibility with network executives. Everyone we met with said they were drawn to his entertaining outbursts and to the complicated, dysfunctional dynamics of our lives—all essential elements for a successful reality show. Jeff's "discovery" instantly spun our show about two actors pursuing fame toward *his* story and the world of real estate.

We soon got a phone call saying Bravo wanted to meet. They told us they were already leaning toward a real estate show, *Million Dollar Listing,* and weren't sure they wanted to air two shows that revolved around the same industry. At the end of the meeting, however, Cori Abraham, a Bravo executive, gave us her card and told us to call her. When we did, she said she believed in *Flipping Out* and was willing to go the extra mile for us. A Skype call was arranged with Lauren Zalaznick, head of the Bravo network, to talk about the show. That call sold *Flipping Out.* Shortly thereafter, they agreed to give us a green light for six episodes—a great start for an unproven show.

My response was bittersweet. On the one hand, I was so happy and excited for the chance we were being given. We put our mind toward a goal and made it happen. On the other hand, after all of the years chasing my dream to become a serious actress, a comedienne and, don't forget, a rapper, I wasn't sure a reality television show about real estate was what I was supposed to be doing.

I was a *successful actress*—or at least that's what I wanted people to believe. If I pursued *Flipping Out*, everyone in Hollywood, along with millions of viewers, would know my secret—the thing I went out of my way to hide—that all I did for a living was work for Jeff Lewis as his assistant.

For Chris, it was even worse because he was the guy hauling Jeff's trash out every day. He didn't want to be on television as a trash-carrying struggling actor/gofer. He actually had an active career, appearing in a major feature film, *How High,* and television shows such as *Spin City* and *Punk'd.* I think in Chris's mind, doing a show like *Flipping Out* was a step down. He didn't want either of us to be humiliated on national television.

He had a point.

When Bravo bought *Flipping Out,* I had to make a choice—my show business version of Sophie's Choice—to give up my passion project and put *The Wannabes* on a shelf or walk away and wait for another shot at stardom. That was really hard.

I needed to figure out if I should do *Flipping Out*. I reached out to my acting coach, Kathleen King, who, since the day I met her, has always helped me find answers by asking me questions. And true to form, instead of telling me what to do, here were her questions:

"What do you really want? Do you want to act?" she asked.

"Yes, I do!"

"Do you think this is something where you can learn about a business you want to be in?"

"Yes, I do!"

"Has Jeff been successful?"

"Yes."

"Have you learned a lot from him so far?"

"Yes."

"Well then, it seems to me you don't have a lot to lose."

If I agreed to do the show, I would be jumping headfirst into unknown territory. I would have to start being honest and willing to do the hard work that would get me to where I wanted to go with my life and career. No more posturing and pretending that I was further along than I actually was. It took courage I didn't think I had to say hello to *Flipping Out* and good-bye to *The Wannabes*. If I sound bitter, I was . . . for about two days.

Although I didn't know it at the time, looking back, this might have been the beginning of the end to my marriage with Chris, too. He was so angry that the networks were gravitating toward Jeff. I struggled to be happy for Jeff and encouraged him to go for it, but Chris begged me to walk away and pursue *The Wannabes*—but I couldn't do it. Kathleen also asked me what would I do if the situation were reversed, how I would want Jeff to support our project. I told Chris how I felt and said I wanted to play it out and see what might come of it. Instead of crumbling in defeat that *The Wannabes* wasn't picked up, I did my best to embrace this new, unexpected opportunity.

> The right people, the ones who really belong in your life, will come to you. And stay.
>
> —WILL SMITH

The first time I met Kathleen was in the summer of 2004 after she saw me perform in a play called *Jewtopia,* in Los Angeles. The actor she had been coaching played my father in the show and he was moving to New York with the production. Before he left, he tried to recommend her to me as an acting coach when I cut him off. I thought, *Awesome! Just what I needed . . . to meet with another acting coach!* I had already worked my way through every great one in the city. But, the next thing I knew, I was in Pasadena at a café sobbing to Kathleen about my not going with the play to New York.

"It's all over," I said.

"You are crazy talented and crazy brave, but you look just crazy because you are out of control. You don't know what you're doing and you have to do something about that attitude and the sneer that goes with it."

No one had ever greeted me like that before or since.

"You need to learn technique and the voice needs a lot of work."

I had given no thought to my voice and its current limitations. All I could think was, *What a bitch.* I had no idea what she was talking about. I was beyond pissed that this complete stranger would speak to me like that, especially after giving what I thought was a supreme performance in *Jewtopia*. But, in actuality, she was right. I really didn't know what I was doing. I had no technique. And no one had ever had the decency or the heart to speak the truth to me like Kathleen did that day. (And she doesn't usually say things like that unless you're paying her.)

Within days of that meeting, I was working regularly with Kathleen. Ours would become one of the most important and life-altering relationships in my life.

There were many times I left Kathleen distraught and filled with anger because I couldn't figure out what she really meant. She speaks in such a way that you have to be engaged and really listening to *hear* the message. Up until I met Kathleen, I did a lot of talking and very little listening. She trained me to listen, which is a critical skill for an actor who wants to be good at their job. And my newfound ability to listen became a big part of what would eventually change my life.

Working with Kathleen was the first time in my career that I genuinely believed someone could see my talent and support it. She is always on my side even if we don't agree on everything. Kathleen helped me to see that all of the time I spent complaining, talking, and *not* doing was actually hurting me. And I felt like she was trying to make things hard for me. Sometimes I still do. But I *can't* argue with her results.

As time went on, I began to think of Kathleen as someone I could trust. Believe me, that says a lot, because at the time I didn't trust anyone! And how could I? I wasn't being truthful about who I was as a person. So why would I think the people around me were?

I'm not a businessman. I'm a business . . . man.

—JAY-Z, RAPPER

Why had I ignored what was right in front of me?

The people who work the hardest often get the best results. That's exactly why the networks loved Jeff. He walked his talk while I walked around making everyone believe I was strong, secure, and happy when I was anything but.

I believe God has an awesome sense of humor, especially when He is trying to browbeat a specific lesson into your head. When He wants to root out a problem in your life, He will keep slapping you with a two-by-four, sometimes literally, until you learn your intended lesson.

MY FIRST CONVERSATION WITH KATHLEEN (CONVERSATIONS WITH AN ALIEN)

1. You never know *what* is going to lead *where*.
2. When something you wanted is given to someone else, realize that your plan B can be a plan A in disguise.
3. Saying "I don't know" is a power position.
4. If at first they think you don't belong, know they can be wrong!
5. You don't see your true self in the mirror; you see it in how you treat yourself and others.
6. Being obsessed with yourself is not the same as seeing yourself.

It was important for me to get it through my head that the one who *really* needed to see me . . . was *me*—and doing *Flipping Out* was my best shot at making that happen.

3

Bloom Where You Are Planted

> Integrate what you believe in every single area of your life. Take your heart to work and ask the most and best of everybody else, too.
>
> —MERYL STREEP

Once the show got off the ground, the rest, as they say, is history. It's clear to anyone who watches our shows that we are in an unusual, highly dysfunctional relationship, yet somehow it seems to work. I want the world to know that I have tremendous love for Jeff Lewis—and I am *not* just making this bold statement because he is making me say it. I swear. (How was that, Jeff?)

I will be forever grateful to Jeff and thankful for the opportunity we have shared together on reality TV. It has taught me a lot. Working with Jeff and doing reality television has forced me to become more self-aware. Granted, much of that has stemmed from tremendous embarrassment, but hey, who knew humiliation would lead me to the life I never knew I wanted?

As a professional, I respect Jeff's work. Simply put, there's no one in the real estate business who can do what Jeff does the way he does it. Jeff has the courage to say the things no one wants to hear, but often needs to hear anyway. I may not always agree or like the way he goes about sharing his point of view, but I admire that he is willing to let you know what he is thinking. And once I stopped being victimized by his choice of words, I actually found myself appreciating that he cared enough about me to say them.

Eventually, most of us will find ourselves in a situation that will require digging down, and I mean way, way down to places you never knew existed within, to find a way to get through working for someone you don't see eye to eye with. Lots of people in the world feel conflicted about people they work with; I totally get it. You don't have to like or even respect your boss, but you do have to be *respectful*—that is, if you plan on continuing to collect a paycheck.

Growing up with my mom was like going to boot camp for all of the bosses I'd encounter throughout my life. She prepared me to never expect a compliment or approval from anyone, which is why I was always so desperate to get it. As I struggled to get my so-called "break" in Hollywood, she encouraged me with her own brand of loving and supportive statements such as: "You made me stay up until ten p.m. for that? You had one scene in that awful program and if I had blinked I would have missed it altogether." Or, when she's feeling really compassionate, I might have gotten something like, "Jennifer, why do you keep ending up on the cutting-room floor?" She says things like this as if she somehow knows the inside lingo of Hollywood.

Flipping Out is now in its seventh season, and although my mom thinks it has gotten funnier, she still believes I am still not getting enough airtime. "You could be in it more. You were barely in it this last year," she recently said. But deep down, I know she's really proud of me and our show. It's a good thing I have such an excellent ability to "reinterpret" her comments, a skill which I credit to Kathleen and therapy—lots and lots of very expensive therapy!

I hate to brag but it's no secret I was a champion at putting my focus in all the wrong places. What I chose to do as survival jobs to be available for my acting auditions says a lot about me. Honestly, it says a lot more about the lessons I needed to learn. Way before meeting Jeff, when I was first starting out as an actress, I took a job at a company called Characters Kids Love. I dressed up as Snow White, Barney, and other characters to entertain at kids' parties. One day I was dressed as Cinderella for a children's hospital event. In a hurry to arrive on time, I forgot to secure my wig. I was doing my thing, entertaining the kids with a story, when one of the children came up from behind and grabbed my hair, really hard. My wig came crashing to the floor, leaving a big matted Greek 'fro exposed for everyone to see.

Yikes!

The kids started screaming "That's not a real Cinderella; she's a fake! She's ugly and fatter then Cinderella, too! We knew something was wrong!"

Then I heard one of the children sob, "Mommy, get that creepy lady out of here!" But for me, the show had to go on! So, I pulled the wig halfway back onto my head and started making balloon animals. "What would you like to have to-day, a rabbit?" I asked. I was doing my best to get through the rest of the time there without crying, but it was a challenge.

"I want you to make Abraham Lincoln!" one of the kids said.

"Oh," I said. "I don't think I can make *him* out of a balloon!"

"Well, a *real* Cinderella could," he said before walking away empty-handed.

Working kids' parties was no joke. They can be rough, especially when a creepy dad once asked me if I could come back to his house and do a Wonder Woman thing for him and his poker buddies. But I always got through it. I'd become thick-skinned pretty fast so I was able to survive the *adventures* I sometimes had to endure. As I did at the Apollo. As I did with my mom. And as I do, *with* Jeff.

Another one of the jobs listed on my colorful résumé was personal assistant to a woman I will refer to as Mrs. Bel Air. I was hired to run errands and do chores and anything else she needed me to do. During my first day on the job, I showed up well prepared, nicely dressed, and ready for a new experience.

Oh, it was an experience, all right!

Mrs. Bel Air came into the kitchen buck naked and said,

"I'm going through menopause. I need you to prepare me a tuna sandwich on white bread with the crusts cut off. Then you will come in and give me a sponge bath."

"Sounds great, I'm going to quickly grab my flip-flops out of the car, okay?" . . . (insert sound of screeching tires)

And then there was Captain Coconut, a character I was hired to portray outside the Captain Coconut toy store at Universal City Walk in Hollywood. (City Walk is a significant tourist attraction and a highly trafficked area due to it being adjacent to Universal Studios.) This was by far the most abusive job I've ever had. I made ten dollars an hour to stand outside the store and lure people in. I wore a pink wig, colorful Jam's board shorts, upside-down spaghetti strainer glasses, neon bouncy trampoline moon shoes, and a voice-activated headset that would squirt water on people when they walked by. I spent eight hours a day jumping up and down saying "Welcome to Captain Coconut's!" Here's a little sampling of the comments I heard every single day:

"Loser!"

"Get a real job!"

"How much are they paying you, fool?"

("Not enough dummy.")

"Guess you didn't go to college."

"Idiot!"

One day, two teenage boys dumped an entire bucket of water on my head from the second story of the shops.

But that didn't make me want to quit.

My then two-year-old nephew Michael (who is now

Scaring children as Captain Coconut—1995.

twenty and a filmmaker) visited me and screamed and cried when he saw me.

I still didn't quit.

And then there was the unforgettable day when a very loud and large woman walked by with her friend. I couldn't see very well out of the spaghetti strainer glasses I wore and I proceeded to squirt water all over her expensive gold lamé blouse. All of a sudden I heard somebody roar, "I'm gonna take that clown down . . ."

I ran for my life through the store, dodging the wind-up toys that were covering the store floor until I finally jumped behind the counter to make a break for the stockroom as my manager intervened. Thankfully, he ended up giving her a twenty-five-dollar gift certificate to the store, which he *deducted from my paycheck.*

I had built up quite a repertoire of off-center jobs that trained me for the eventual coping I would need to do as Jeff's assistant. You might even say these early positions made me highly qualified for the job with Jeff.

At first, I used silence to cope with Jeff and his behavior. But then one day I realized that so much of his anger toward me wasn't about me, at all. It was about *his* life, *his* insecurities, and *his* personal challenges. Hey, we all have them, even if we don't like to admit it or show them like he does. This epiphany was like a lightbulb going on in my head, and suddenly I understood that *I* wasn't the cause of Jeff's misery any more then *he* was the cause of mine. And even though there's been many times when we've both wanted to go our own way, we've hung in there and continued to work together— for more than ten years, now. I suppose that means that neither of us are quitters. It is our work ethic that has kept us together.

While most people crumble under Jeff's passion, I haven't because I get him and he gets me. Working for him let me see the payoff of choosing to go from victim to victor. Living a life based on being a victim, the "what do you think of me" mentality, was miserable and changing that thinking has helped me become a victor! To me, being a victor meant undertaking the process of getting over my obsession with myself. Hearing everything from an off-kilter perspective, I validated critics— those who did or didn't have credentials.

Jeff has been a great training ground for making changes as well as surviving whatever life throws my way. Sure, his insults have been rough at times, but after surviving Captain Coconut, the naked lady in Bel Air, and performing at those brutal kids' parties, I'm able to endure just about anything! What others have seen with Jeff as being rude and crude, for me it's been just another day at the office. (Usually . . .)

And besides, who am I going to complain to?

When most people have an issue with their bosses at work, they can take it to the head of Human Resources and file some sort of complaint.

But not me.

Why?

Because I *am* the HR department at Jeff Lewis Design. And believe me, at Jeff Lewis Design it's a full-time job, even with such a small staff.

To tackle that part of the business, I had a lot to learn. Even now, I'm still trying to find ways to bring a more streamlined and professional approach to Jeff's business. When the HR department is only one person, as it is at Jeff Lewis Design, things are a bit different. You don't have many options. In my case, I've had to get very good at talking to myself. (And I'm sure you realize by now, that I *do* have a talent for that!) If I have a problem, I report it to myself. There is no committee. Whenever I do write up a formal complaint, I'm usually called "mom," "buzz-kill," or "bitch."

In contrast, when I attend the annual Old Spaghetti Factory meeting for its employees, the situation is completely different. The head of Human Resources told me they go to seminars and teach their managers how to respect the employees, customers, and everyone else associated with the business. Complaints are filed and discussed, and finally reviewed by a committee where they are resolved.

Wow.

When I shared my experiences with the head of HR for Old Spaghetti Factory, I'm sure she thought I was just joking. But I wasn't. I was dead serious. We're a small office. Our atmosphere is much less formal than a larger company or corporation. So in a way, the potential for claims of harassment are greater. Everything is magnified. When I asked her for advice on dealing with interoffice issues, her response was simply, "I wouldn't know where to begin! Maybe you should write a letter . . ."

So I did, you know, just to see what it might look like:

Dear Director of Human Resources,

Where do I begin? My boss, with great charm, often uses our office as a vehicle to embarrass his employees. Do you have any research proving that the feelings of employees matter in the workplace? Can negative reinforcement affect the quality of productivity? Is there any agreed upon nonunion procedure for bathroom and lunch breaks?

Please define the term sexual harassment.

Ditto employer/employee boundaries.

Signed,

Ms. Kick A. Pulos

Dear Ms. Kick A. Pulos,

As head of human resources, I unfortunately do not have access to the data you requested. My suggestion at this time, unless major boundaries are crossed, is to suck it up and be happy you have a job.

Signed,
Ms. Jennifer Pulos

Dear Ms. Jennifer Pulos,

Please define major boundaries.

Signed,
Ms. Kick A. Pulos

Dear Ms. Kick A. Pulos,

That information will be forthcoming.

Signed,
Ms. Jennifer Pulos

Something I've realized over time is to recognize *when* I'm doing a great job, and to validate myself. You can't get blood from a stone, so expecting your boss to understand what it feels like to be you is a waste of time. I grew up in a home with parents who didn't gush over their children's accomplishments—big or small. I can't expect something from someone if he or she isn't capable of giving it to me. And that applies to both my work and my personal life. It's an unrealistic expectation to think that the people around you are always going to be able to do what you need them to, to always feed your needs, especially when they are working on their own lives and their own issues. You can't ask a cow to play the guitar.

Another thing I've come to realize is that very often strong women seem to have an especially hard time in the workplace. They're often minimized for characteristics and traits that would otherwise be seen as an asset in men. (A strong man is respected; a strong woman is often seen as being a ball buster.) With all of the experience I've gained over the years, I've learned four surefire ways to deal with a boss when he or she is being difficult:

- Ignore them when they act up.
- Be effective, not emotional.
- End bad behavior.
- Make the difficult and disciplined choice not to pay attention and stay focused on the work you have to do.

For the most part, whenever someone is trying to test me, I've learned to keep my mouth shut and not talk back. If you've ever watched our show, you've probably noticed several times where I say nothing.

"You are a terrible assistant."

Silence.

"Why do I even have an assistant when I do everything myself?"

Silence.

"If this job is so horrible, there's the door."

Silence.

Even though, at times, I'd love to be standing my ground, defending my actions, or having my say, I find keeping quiet usually diffuses a heated situation. The person being difficult doesn't have anything to react to, anything to feed on . . . including you.

If you've ever argued with someone who has to be right all of the time, you know they won't stop until you concede. Even if you're right, you'll usually lose the argument because that type of personality absolutely, positively, *has to be right all of the time*, so why prolong the agony by fighting back? In many tense situations, I stay quiet on purpose and let the situation run its course. These days I try my best to not give anyone the satisfaction of seeing me respond with so much as a half-cracked smile or raised eyebrows when they are acting up. That's a reward for their bad behavior, and I don't want to give it!

I like to think of myself as a babysitter who won't stoop to the level of the child I am caring for by engaging in their bad behavior. Let's face it, when someone goes off on you, they're usually just acting out. I don't see how it's any different from a child having a temper tantrum.

To be fair, there have been many times throughout my professional career when I've let my various bosses get to me, and even found myself occasionally pouring gasoline on the fire as my own way of coping.

Yeah, that didn't work quite as well as the silence thing does. When I was younger, I did that a lot. I would take the bait and was a magnet for chaos. Or I'd create my own. I looked for drama and didn't care where or how I found it. But none of that ever made me feel any better! It took me a while, but over time, I learned that engaging in an angry, heated exchange never works out to anyone's advantage. (Okay, maybe it did, but only for a moment.)

I once left a phone number for a subcontractor at Jeff's office and didn't discover my mistake until we were en route to the job site. The number was easy enough to get, but Jeff wanted the number *right away*! I spent fifteen minutes listening to a rush of words about how stupid and irresponsible it was of me to leave the phone number at home. There was a time in my life when I might have hung on those words. I might have even believed them to be true. These days, those types of negative statements rarely get to me or rile me up.

When Jeff finished, I simply responded by saying, "Mistakes happen."

He replied, "Mistakes *don't* happen if you're good at your job."

This was an instance where staying silent worked well. I knew I could easily get the number, but at that point, it wasn't about the number anymore.

I've spent years allowing other people the opportunity to "help" me feel bad about myself. Of course, you can't stop someone from forming a negative opinion of you. But just because a person doesn't like you or doesn't approve of something you've done, they're not necessarily right, and their perspective is not necessarily accurate.

Maybe you have to look at your boss or the other people around you with a clearer lens. And if things do get rough, holding some type of grudge for the way you've been treated really does make it nearly impossible for things to ever get better. If there's been tension between you and someone else, step back and do a reality check. Ask yourself or others if you're acting negative. And don't fear the response. If you're running around with a chip on your shoulder, drop the attitude—and I mean fast—or before you know it, you'll be working the unemployment line.

With a demanding boss, there will often be something they will zero in on to create havoc. It can be something as simple as not lining up the water bottles in the refrigerator perfectly straight with the label side facing out or the way you deal with a vendor for not shipping an order on time, which isn't your fault, but it is your problem. I find the best way to take my thoughts off the negativity that sometimes swirls about is to focus on something productive.

Whenever I feel a rampage coming on in the office, I go back to my desk, the job site, or wherever I need to be to do my work. Instead of creating a firestorm, I do the following:

1. Take a deep breath.
2. Identify the problem.
3. Keep the focus on solving the problem.
4. Recognize that even a small step in the right direction can change everything.
5. Remember that problems are the breakfast of champions!

In other words, I get effective, not emotional!

Tomorrow I could lose my job. That's a fact. But I'll never lose the knowledge I've gained in design, building, and real estate. I try to focus on thinking like that to keep me inspired. Plus, I remind myself often that I love the people I work with—including Jeff and Zoila, who always says what everyone else is thinking.

I've learned that a boss is not a parent or a dispenser of unconditional love. I no longer go into work with the expectation of looking for compliments, praise, or acknowledgment for the things I've done. I know I'm doing my job well, and don't sit back waiting for someone to tell me that in order to feel worthy. Your boss has a job to do and you have a job to do.

One thing I discovered on the job is that the more

demanding I got in my need to be praised or receive credit for the things I'd done, the less I got it and the more disappointed I became. It was a vicious cycle, one that didn't serve me on the job or as a struggling up-and-coming wannabe actress. Thinking back, I bet that if I had just prepared myself to have a great audition regardless of the outcome, then probably I would have landed more roles earlier. But at that time, my ego was way out of check and I believed my talent was huge. It was all I needed to succeed. In the early days, I thought I could go in and just wing it, and someone would simply hand me a role because I was me! I was looking for someone to give me a career, a director to give me a performance, connected friends to give me jobs. It was a theme that kept repeating itself. (Repeatedly, Kathleen called me a "get monkey" and I would give her the finger. Actually, two fingers as I used both hands.)

Though I didn't really know this at the time, when it came to everything I was doing, I spent years running instead of learning to bloom where I was planted. But I finally learned the true meaning of that phrase. Some people attribute this quote to the Bible while others say it's merely a gardening tip. I translate it like this: If you don't have what you feel is the perfect home, perfect relationship, or the perfect job make the best of what you have while you can. Blooming where you are planted can lead you to a much better future.

When your focus and commitment are off, don't expect things to work.

Case in point: When Jeff's design business really began to skyrocket, he was offered the opportunity to design the "kitchen of the year" for *House Beautiful*. The editor of the magazine asked Jeff to come to New York to design a kitchen that would be on display at 30 Rock . . . an address written in my heart since 1975. It's a huge honor and was a milestone for Jeff and his career. I thought he would ask me to come to New York to help.

He didn't.

I offered to pay my own way.

He still said no.

I felt rejected and upset by what I felt was his dismissal of my contributions that had helped get him to this exciting place. Jeff knew all these years that while I was working for him, I still wanted a full-time career as an actress. With only one foot in on most everything I was doing, how could I be giving him my all? His way of letting me know that was to exclude me from going to New York. I accepted his decision, but I wasn't happy about it. Yet, I still had to go to work and put on a happy face. But Jeff finally realized how upset I was and that I actually understood where he was coming from, and he changed his mind.

"I thought about it and I would really like you to come to New York," he said.

"Really?"

"Yes, and don't make me change my mind. And whatever you do . . . no hugs."

So of course I hugged him . . . maybe too hard.

On day three of our week at Rockefeller Center, Jeff threw out his back and was unable to attend a few of the events. I was asked to represent Jeff Lewis Design. In the end, it worked out that I was there and he was thankful and appreciative. I believe Jeff knows that no matter what, he can count on me to have his back—even his bad back.

It took me a while, but I finally realized that if I wanted to achieve the kind of results I was seeking, I had to make a commitment to the things I said, wanted, and cared about, which changed everything.

MY CRASH COURSE IN COMMITMENT

1. Stop the talk. Start the walk.
2. Stop saying "I can't find the time." Find it.
3. Do the things you don't want to do to make the things you want, happen.
4. Find happiness in the little victories along the way.
5. There is always another mountain, another obstacle. Make peace with that.

I wasted so many years looking at the glass as half empty. Now, thankfully, I see it as half full.

4

Nanny-Cam Diaries

> Keep your mouth closed and let your eyes listen.
>
> —LIL WAYNE, RAPPER

The first season of *Flipping Out* was only six episodes. Our ratings were good enough to get us picked up for a second season. It also got Jeff and I booked on *Nightline*. I had gone from being a struggling actress, to an unknown assistant, to sitting on the set of one of the most popular late-night network news programs—talking about our little show. At the time, Jeff had bought the house that Paris Hilton had been renting but had moved from after he made the purchase. Her mail continued to be delivered there long after she was gone. I confess one particular package was impossible to resist because of the return label. So I opened it. It was sexy lingerie. C'mon! Paris Hilton? The girl who says to "live every day like it's your birthday." At the end of the *Nightline* interview, overcome with this top-tier recognition, I announced I had stolen Paris Hilton's panties. The host's face was one of total horror. There were a few seconds when he seemed at a loss for words. It wasn't my best moment, but it sure did get something I longed for—attention!

After the show aired, I got an immediate call from my mother.

"Oh, Jennifer, talking about stealing panties? How am I going to explain this to the ladies in the church bookstore on Sunday? You better go to confession."

Just my luck, she managed to watch the right channel this time.

Not long after my great panty heist revelation, I appeared on an MSNBC news show with Jeff to talk about the housing market. I went to the studio unaware that I'd be asked to sit in on the interview. I was wearing a short white dress that was very sheer under the bright studio lights, so I quickly removed my underwear so no one could see them on camera. I was horrified to discover that we would be sitting on a stool, where one wrong move could turn me into the Sharon Stone of home design. Luckily, I kept my knees locked tight and got through the interview without anyone realizing I had done it commando.

Coincidentally, the naked truth about my marriage was about to be exposed. Although Chris had doubts about the show when it started, by the second season he had decided to work hard and embrace the experience. I believed he was all in. By then, Chris had been promoted to house manager, and Jeff had hired a second assistant to work under Chris. We were on a major cable network and *Flipping Out* was being watched by millions of viewers—and growing—every week. Everything was going great—or so I thought.

Unbeknownst to me, Jeff had some suspicions about Chris and his commitment to work. Zoila, Jeff's faithful housekeeper, had taken Jeff aside and privately told him that she caught Chris going into Jeff's office when he wasn't there. Chris's job required him to do many things, but there was nothing that would have kept him on Jeff's private computer for extended periods. Jeff had always made it abundantly clear to everyone who worked at his home/office that no one should ever use his personal computer. There was no gray area on this. And I began to notice that Jeff was repeating this rule more often than usual, as if he was dropping hints to everyone that he knew something we didn't. Of course, I couldn't imagine the real reason he kept mentioning the same thing over and over, but it was obvious something was going on.

Chris also began asking to leave work early more often than usual. Jeff began to have suspicions that Chris wasn't actually going on auditions. But I gave Jeff my word that Chris would never lie. In the privacy of our home, I asked Chris if he was doing anything out of line, or using Jeff's computer when he wasn't supposed to. He assured me he would never do anything to disrespect Jeff like that, and I believed him. Chris must have known that Zoila watched everything that goes on around Jeff's house. We all knew she is his eyes and ears in his absence, but I guess Chris never believed Zoila would say anything to Jeff. He guessed wrong. She felt that Chris was neglecting his responsibilities and taking advantage of his position. To confirm Zoila's accusations, Jeff installed a hidden security camera so he could see for himself what Chris was doing.

Jeff never said a word to anyone about the cameras. Besides, we were all so used to cameras being around during the day filming *Flipping Out,* that no one would have thought anything of it if they were spotted. Jeff collected tapes for weeks before he came to me with what he saw.

Thankfully, Jeff chose to break the news to me in private about what he'd recorded. And when he finally did take me aside, it was as if he could no longer keep what he knew to himself. Out of concern for my reaction, he told the Bravo camera crew to stay outside while he and I spoke. I was nervous because he'd never done that before. I wasn't sure what was happening.

He explained that Chris had been spending hours using his personal computer for things unrelated to work. To this day, Jeff has spared me the details of everything he discovered and to be candid, I really didn't want to know. What I do know is Zoila was right—Chris was not working the way he said he was. I refused to accept that Chris would ever betray Jeff in that way, even swearing on my life that there had to be some misunderstanding. But there wasn't.

Jeff told me about the hidden camera and then pointed to it up in the corner of his office where we were standing, and explained that everything had been recorded and documented.

I fell to the floor in total disbelief. It felt as if someone had cut my strings. And then I began to cry.

Upon hearing me wail, Zoila came into the room and held me as I sobbed.

"Please don't ruin his life!" I pleaded with Jeff.

I couldn't believe what was happening. I know in my heart Jeff took zero satisfaction or had a single moment of joy in breaking this news to me. He felt terrible. But he also knew if he didn't show me the proof he had, I would never have believed him.

He was right about that, too. There was no denying the evidence.

A part of me wondered why Jeff let this go on as long as he did, but I also knew he had to protect his business and his privacy. So he had to be careful and be sure before telling me what had been going on. When I calmed down, Jeff said he was going to fire Chris, and out of respect for me, he wanted to tell me first.

"You know I have to fire him, right?" Jeff said, stating the obvious.

This was one of those unforgettable dark moments where reality turned into insanity. I looked up at the hidden camera and wondered, "Is this what I helped construct? Did I want to be famous so bad that I allowed this to happen?"

In an ironic twist of fate, earlier that same week, Chris and I had been told that there was a possibility that the original show based on our *Wannabes* concept could go forward after all. We were excited by the prospect, but suddenly the bottom had fallen out from beneath my feet. I never saw it coming.

I got into my car and drove to the safety of Kathleen's house. In that moment, it was the only place I could think of going. Home was out of the question. I was too mad, hurt, and vulnerable. I don't really remember the drive. It was as if I was having an out-of-body experience. I couldn't believe what was happening. There were a million questions racing through my mind as I drove:

Who had I been married to?
Who was I?
What would I do?
Where would I go?
Did I still have any trust for Chris?

Despite the evidence presented, everything inside of me still wanted to protect Chris. When I got to Kathleen's I was beyond a mess. I definitely went into the ugly cry.

Knowing he'd been caught, Chris called me repeatedly, but I couldn't talk. I was paralyzed by my fear and hurt.

In a panic, Chris spoke to Kathleen and asked what he should do. Her response was simply, "Show up, Chris." Chris needed to man up and deal with the chaos he created.

It took me a day or two to actually face Chris. It felt like my whole world had been destroyed. When we finally spoke, I told Chris to temporarily move out so the cameras from our show couldn't capture what was happening in our home. I did not want to make an awful situation worse. In that moment I thought, *I'll leave the show and we will go back to selling The Wannabes.*

Chris was my husband, and I was his wife who had taken a vow to stand by his side, for better or for worse. This being said, I was relieved that Chris was gone for a few days. I figured by the time he got back, everything would have blown over and we could start our new life together.

I had no idea what would come next.

I went back to work, hoping I could face the inevitable humiliation with some shred of dignity. It was hard, but I ploughed through, business as usual. By the time I walked into the office Jeff was back to his old self. In fact, he warned me that in certain types of stressful situations, he can sometimes say inappropriate things as his own means of coping. He apologized in advance for his verbal Tourette's.

"You know, if this doesn't work out, there are plenty of guys I can fix you up with! My tree trimmer is single," Jeff said with a smirk. I knew he was joking, trying to lighten up the mood, but I couldn't muster up enough strength to crack a smile through my obvious and excruciating pain. I hadn't really thought about life without my husband. I mean, why would I? It never occurred to me.

The producers wanted to interview me that afternoon to

capture how I was feeling. A part of me felt obligated to give them what they wanted, but another part felt like I needed some privacy to deal with my feelings. It felt as though a tornado had ripped through my world with no warning. For the most part, the crew didn't even want to be a part of my misery, but they had their job to do, as did I. When reality television becomes brutally real, it's devastating. My most private moments were now everyone's public information. I had no idea what I had signed up for. I even wondered if I was somehow being punished for what I had set into motion by wanting this kind of attention so badly.

As the days passed, things cleared and I suddenly felt extremely betrayed. Who had I been with for all of those years? I didn't even know the man Jeff described to me that horrible day.

I felt so sick thinking about the humiliation and backlash that would surely come. My family would suffer, his family would suffer, our colleagues would suffer and, despite all the fallout, my initial reaction was to protect him.

A few days later, Chris came home and was ready to talk. I was confused and angry. Maybe I wasn't ready to move on so fast. I needed time and space to think it all through so I went to stay with my family for a couple of days. I asked Chris to seek counseling from our Spiritual Father at our church, someone who had counseled hundreds of marriages. He knew us pretty well, so I often turned to him throughout our marriage for his insights. This time was no exception.

When we met, he asked Chris if there was another woman involved. Of course, Chris said there wasn't. Our priest is a very wise man. He told Chris that if he had any desire to make our relationship work, everything needed to come out into the open. Chris held his ground, insisting there wasn't someone else in his life. I wasn't sure I believed him.

What *was* my future with Chris? This was a question I had never really asked myself, until he was fired from the show. After the counseling session I offered to do whatever it would take to save our marriage, even if it meant leaving the show. Chris told me that wasn't the solution. He promised to get another job and committed to doing whatever it would take to make things work. Deep down, I believe Chris told me to stay on *Flipping Out* because even though I didn't have an inkling of the truth, he already knew he was leaving me for good.

Right after that meeting, Chris flew to Las Vegas to do a job and was gone again for a couple of days. Even though things were rough between us, I looked forward to his return and trying to salvage whatever was left of our marriage. When Chris arrived home we went to a birthday party together. It was a small gathering of eight good friends who were all in the know about what had happened. Chris assured everyone there that we were going to work things out—get counseling and try to grow from this experience. He readily admitted that he'd made a terrible mistake and spoke about how marriages go through ups and downs. Since he was no longer involved in the show, there was no reason to doubt the authenticity of what he was saying as there were no cameras rolling—just close friends having drinks and a celebration dinner.

Even though I felt betrayed, I definitely wanted to be with Chris and thought we could work things out with time and counseling. So we decided that night to stay together and give our marriage a chance.

The following weekend would be our first date night together since the illusion of our happy marriage had been shattered. I was excited and eagerly anticipated a romantic evening. When Chris came home that night, he walked through the door and almost immediately blurted out something like, "I'm leaving you. I was never really attracted to you. I have loved you more than anyone else, but I'm supposed to be alone. I am not meant to be married. But I want you to know that I still want to be best buddies." He really did think we could still work together. But I didn't see it that way. You can't be respected and trusted with someone's dreams if you have deceived them.

"Besides, you'll probably end up with some doctor!" he said, trying to lighten the moment. I didn't see the humor at all.

I stood in our living room in tears, listening to what he had to say, with our two dogs at my feet. I looked down at our pug Janet, who had a "get him out of here" snarl on her sweet face. Then she pounced on Chris—as it would turn out to be, for the very last time. "She's so stupid," he said. "She doesn't even know what's happening." Looking back, I'm not so sure he wasn't talking about me. Janet—named after Janet Reno—is one smart bitch. I can't say the same about her owner.

The next day I called our Spiritual Father and I asked his advice about what I should do. This is a man who does whatever he can to help make marriages work, but this time he told me to have Chris write down the following sentence on a piece of paper: "I don't want to be married," and anything else he might have to say and then have him sign it.

"When he does, you are done. It is over," he said.

He told me that if I ever had a second thought about going back to the marriage, I should go back and read the paper— that it would help bring me clarity. Chris's letter was only a few sentences long and he typed it in a very small font. It clearly stated he didn't want to be obligated to me. He signed it with ease. And I accepted it with heartache. But our priest was right. Every time I looked at the letter, I knew my marriage to Chris was over forever.

I am a big believer in life taking you on the journey that you're supposed to be on. Although I knew it would be painful and scary to be on my own, I also understood it would be far worse if I allowed this kind of behavior to be tolerated and accepted going forward. Something bigger than I can explain carried me through my pain with the hope that there was someone who would love me, though at times I wondered if anyone would ever love me.

I had originally thought losing my marriage meant I was a failure. I was wrong. I don't know the reason why Chris and

I came into each other's lives—I may never know. But I do know that for whatever reason the ten years we were together were meant to be.

Ya gotta fuck up before you get your shit right.

—KID INK (BRIAN TODD COLLINS),

L.A. RAPPER

I promise that even if you don't know it right now, the pain, suffering, humiliation, devastation, panic, fear, and loneliness that may be holding you back, can actually be the road that will lead you to your dreams. I was desperately afraid to be alone and on my own, but I was willing to go through that fear to get to the other side. I really didn't have a choice. I certainly wasn't going to die of a broken heart, but there were days I felt like that was a possibility.

I was in a lot pain for months after Chris left. And things didn't get any easier during that time. I was afraid to sleep and be alone on any level. One of the days Chris was moving out, I noticed a collectable action figure of a man hanging from a tree outside my window. I don't know if Chris intentionally left it there or if he hung it on the tree when he was moving out and forgot to take it or if it was something else. What I do know is that it totally freaked me out. From that day on, I worried almost every time I walked through my front door.

Most people who go through trying times or tremendous hurt often refer to that period as a blur, and that's how it felt. I think it's why most women can't remember the pain of childbirth. We must be genetically wired to forget agony, or we'd never have more than one child or allow ourselves to love again after heartbreak.

Even after the dust settled in my private life, I still dreaded the episodes that would make my worst secret public. We film our show several months in advance of the airdate, so I had plenty of time to lick my wounds before they were sliced wide open once again. I was paranoid about the show airing and how the story would be told. Especially since I have no control over what the final show looks like, what scenes go in, and which are left out. I prayed every single day that Bravo and our producers would protect me, but I didn't have a clue of how it would all play out.

Of course, I watched the episodes leading up to that particular show and could finally see the truth about my relationship with Chris. I felt even worse about myself and our life together. I missed all of the signs, mostly because I wanted to. For example, I always thought Chris was an animal lover, until I watched him push one of Jeff's dogs. No wonder my sweet Janet wanted me to kick Chris to the curb! My dog sensed what I simply refused to see.

When the fateful day arrived to watch this now infamous episode, I was with Jeff and his ex-partner Ryan, at Ryan's home. They did their best to show me compassion and to be sympathetic, but it didn't make the viewing any easier. I ran out of their house bawling after the first few minutes. I couldn't watch another second of that agonizing episode, and have never tried again since. I left Ryan's house and ambled up the street, trying to escape my feelings. I began to jog before breaking into an angry full-out sprint—much like the runs I used to take when I was at UCLA. About a mile down the road, one of the producers found me. I was frozen in fear. Just when I thought I was moving on, the show had pulled me right back in.

For ten years, I was completely convinced that I had been in a happy, healthy relationship. Of course, looking back, now I suspect Chris wanted to get caught. I believe that he was fed up with being on the show and didn't know any other way to get out. Worst of all, he chose to let this emotional landslide unfold on national television.

I never thought I would get divorced or that my marriage would fail. It had been a huge fear of mine, especially seeing my mom never truly recover from hers. I vowed that it would never happen to me. And then, suddenly, there I was. I had become my mother and was publicly living out my worst nightmare. It would have been asinine and egotistical to think I had no role in the outcome. I had to take personal responsibility for my contribution to any dysfunctional relationship I chose to be in. I also had to take a step back and try to realize the other person's perspective.

Jeff once told me that when it came to Chris, I needed to

get the earphones out of my ears. At the time, I had no idea what he meant. After watching the second season of *Flipping Out,* it made perfect sense. I'd been blocking out all of the noise and disguising it as beautiful music. Sadly, it took a produced and edited television show in front of my face for me to open my eyes and finally see what I had been blinded to for so long.

THE NANNY-CAM MADE ME LEARN

1. You can fail, be betrayed, and totally humiliated on national television and not die.
2. The worst-case scenario often isn't.
3. People who disrespect boundaries at work are probably doing the same thing at home.
4. I had no idea what to look for in a life partner.
5. I am not as smart as my dog.

5

Go Toward the Hit

I think I can
I think I can
I think I can . . .

—WATTY PIPER (ARNOLD MUNK)
THE LITTLE ENGINE THAT COULD

When America watched my marriage unfold on national television, what most people didn't know was that Chris had actually left me once before that final breakdown of our relationship. In 2004, about four years into our marriage, he came to me and confessed that "he couldn't be married anymore," much like he would do years later. The weekend before he dropped this first bombshell, Chris and I had gone to a friend's wedding and had what I thought was a great weekend together. But there was a weird incident where I caught Chris walking another woman back to her room. At the time, though,

I didn't think too much about it. Looking back, I can recall a little flirtation going on, but it was a wedding, people were tipsy, and I shrugged it off as no big deal.

My relationship with Chris seemed fine. We were still affectionate and didn't really fight a lot, so I didn't understand where this confession was coming from. The wedding must have brought something up for him that I was unaware of. I really had no idea what he was talking about when he said he didn't want to be married anymore. Here comes that two-by-four again! Whack!

"I just can't do it. There is no counseling or anything we can do that is going to repair it. I'm done." This was the only explanation Chris gave that day after the wedding.

"What did I do?" I asked through my tears, but he wouldn't answer.

Surely I'd done something to bring this on. Why on earth would he be pulling away if I hadn't?

I let a few days go by. After giving it a lot of thought I decided I would fight as hard as I could to salvage our relationship. I begged Chris to go to counseling, which he agreed to do on the condition we sought the help of someone outside of our church. We found a wonderful therapist who was a straight shooter and she got right to the point. When she asked each of us if the other was the right person for us, I quickly responded, "I will do whatever it takes." Of course, I didn't notice that I didn't say, "Yes."

I was well aware of my deeply rooted abandonment issues that resulted from my father leaving my mother, so my greatest fear in life was having my husband leave me. Worse, I feared that if Chris left, he would go on to become famous and I'd be all on my own as a once barely famous wannabe. Isn't that pathetic! In my heart, and as his wife, I wanted Chris to make it as an actor but only if I was in control of the path. How awful is that? I wasn't being fair to either of us, but I knew he was fabulously talented and I was controlling and jealous. There, I said it.

When the therapist asked Chris what the chances were that we could work things out, I think his response was, "About ten percent."

I saw that answer as a good thing because at least there was still hope. (Okay, lock me up.)

Throughout our weekly therapy sessions, I felt like Humpty Dumpty trying to piece back together the frayed threads of my marriage. I wanted things to work. I deluded myself with the thought that perhaps he was just confused, that he had the "seven-year itch" three years early, or any other excuse I could conjure up to justify his desire to leave. It was all so desperate. I promised to change, to do better, to do or be anything he asked.

I completely ignored the fact that Chris was part of the marriage. He also had feelings and needs. And he did say that he didn't want to be in the game, but I wasn't listening.

Less than a month after he left, I was in my car when I saw Chris walking down the street. When he waved, I pulled over to say hi and asked him if he wanted to talk. He did. He said he had made a mistake by leaving me. In that moment, I felt like I had dodged a bullet. I had no idea the gun was still loaded and would fire again someday. Still, the first few weeks we were back together, things felt tentative and I was uncertain of what the future would bring. But as time went on, we eased back into our old comfortable existence. I was deaf to any bells of warning and *holy hell there were bells*:

Ding—If he tells you he wants to be a player, listen.

Ding—10% is what I pay my agent, not what I want from a life partner.

Ding—Trying to control another person is not the same as loving them.

It was around this same time that I was first cast in *Jewtopia*, I was sharing my role with another actress who was there before I came on board. Once I was added to the roster she left the show to do other acting jobs so I took over our role full time. About a year later, the play was headed to New York as an off-Broadway show. I was so excited to be going to New York as a working actress. I quickly found an apartment that Chris and I would move into during the run. It was the perfect fresh start we needed. And, I thought this would be my big break because *Saturday Night Live* was filmed in New York and surely Lorne Michaels would come see me in *Jewtopia*.

Um, no.

Unfortunately, my rising star off-Broadway never came to pass. When the other actress heard about the show moving to New York, she stepped in and said she wanted to go as the lead actress and was not interested in sharing the role with me. She demanded that I be ousted, and she won. The producers chose her over me—so once again, I was like a Weeble. I wobbled and still got back up.

Chris didn't take the news quite as well as I did. In fact, he confronted the other actress about her last-minute decision.

"I got f***ed over so many times in my career that it's my turn to f*** other people over!" He told me that was her response.

After that loss, for a while, life got back to normal. Ironically, even though I didn't get the chance to move to New York, Chris and I were both cast in a movie called *Manhattan Minutiae*. Chris was the male lead and I was his best girl "friend." It was like old times. Of course, the elation was only temporary. Sadly, I didn't know our reconciliation would only last a few years and the same problems would eventually resurface on national television. I wasn't naïve or stupid. I was in love and couldn't or wouldn't recognize the truth about my marriage until it was exposed on *Flipping Out*.

So, after the infamous nanny cam show aired, it took a little while to get used to strangers writing or stopping me on the street to offer comfort, support, and kind words of hope. They didn't know me, but they witnessed my pain and humiliation and offered their compassion and care anyway.

Jenni Pulos

These letters and encounters were very important and the unconditional love from these people helped me get me through a horrifying time. Bravo and NBC had actually sent me to see a therapist before the show aired to make sure I would understand how my experiences would make other people feel. I had been forewarned about their reactions and was for the most part ready for whatever came my way. Although I didn't know the people who reached out to me, they felt as though they knew me, and in many ways, they do.

I now understand that what Jeff did wasn't cruel. He was just opening my eyes to the truth. I may not have liked his methods, but I can't be angry about where it ultimately led me. And for that, I will forever be grateful.

Even though I was in the midst of an almost debilitating depression, I knew I didn't deserve to stay humiliated forever. I knew that no matter what came my way, I had to hold my head up and refuse to speak negatively about Chris or the situation as it unfolded.

I had to stay focused, which wasn't easy. I was aching to get off the train.

So what do you do?

Instead of getting off the train, no matter how much that out-of-the-way station is winking at you, stay on it for the ride—the journey. In my case, it felt as if someone had their foot in my back holding me down on that damned train because my nature was to leap from it regardless of how fast it was rolling along.

Even when I wanted to hide in my bed and pull the covers over my head, I couldn't. I still had to show up for work because there were three months of filming left. I was forced to keep walking and I thank God every day for that. It was a blessing because I could have fallen into a deep depression if I didn't have something to go toward or the support of friends, strangers, and many others who propped me up whenever I was falling down. Sometimes we need someone to simply be there . . . not to fix anything or do anything in particular, but just to let us feel we are supported, cared about . . . and yes, SEEN.

I remember one of my blog entries on the Bravo Web site was simply, "Nobody except the people involved understand the dynamics of a marriage. I hope you understand that I can't say a lot at this time." Clearly those words struck a chord with our viewers because I received fifteen hundred responses, most filled with love and support for what I was going through and expressing all that I couldn't bring myself to say aloud. The messages that bashed Chris only made me feel worse because I knew he must have been getting his share of negative reaction and I didn't want him to suffer any more than I knew he already was.

My family was also extremely supportive, but when it came time to really being there for me, sadly, they couldn't completely do it. I really believe they wanted to be there, but sometimes when people go through a hard time or suffer some type of loss, loved ones often retreat because they don't know how to respond or handle things. People can't stand being in hospitals or they freak out at the thought of someone they love suffering so they disappear instead of showing up. When Kathleen saw people pulling away from me, she sat me down and said this was the most important time in my life to "go toward the hit."

"Go toward the hit" is a phrase Kathleen uses often in her work. In an acting scene, going toward the hit is about your ability to perceive what is going on and the caliber of your response. A less-sensitive or skilled actor can shut down, close up, and fall back on automatic pilot. A courageous actor will go toward the hit. Their body physically opens up and you feel their emotion every bit as much as you see it.

In life, when you go toward the hit, you make a choice to show up in a way perhaps others couldn't or wouldn't. By doing this, it makes you a willing participant in your life—something I had to learn the hard way. You don't create hits, but when they come your way, you deal with them head-on and keep going. Deal, and move on.

When it came to my breakup with Chris, my ability to go toward the hit was tested big time. I felt the pain every time he said he didn't love me or wasn't attracted to me. Though there were many moments I should have walked away, I didn't because I was unaware of what he really wanted from our relationship in the first place. Every failed relationship cannot just be the other person's fault. To be certain, the demise of my relationship with Chris wasn't just about the things he did—I played a huge hand in sabotaging it, too. And I recognize that now. For me to face that realization meant I'd have to go toward the hit—hard. I'm not saying that what I did was heroic. In fact, it was far from it.

Early on, I decided there would be no bashing Chris publicly for what he had done or said about me. I certainly had the forum to do it, with cameras rolling every day. I could have, but I didn't. Even in the darkest moments, I chose to protect him. And now, as I share my story with you, I am only sharing my perspective—what it felt like for me. Chris and I have never talked about what this experience was like for him, but I can say with great certainty that I don't think it was pleasant for him either. He had to learn his own lessons—lessons that hopefully changed his life for the better every bit as much as my lessons changed mine.

A couple of years ago I still couldn't talk about the breakup of my marriage. The only way I know I can feel good about any of this is to help those of you reading my story, those of you who might be going through something similar, to believe that this, too, shall pass. It would eventually take a lot of help to heal my broken heart, to learn to trust, and to stop thinking I would never be loved again. You cannot avoid being heartbroken in life. God does not give you any more than you can handle. I believe that.

6

Over and *Beginning* Are the Same Word

> Educating the mind without educating the heart is no education at all.
>
> —ARISTOTLE (HE'S GREEK, TOO)

When I agreed to do a reality television show it never occurred to me that my pain and struggles would become someone else's entertainment. As I was healing from my breakup, Kathleen once said to me, "Don't block it, go ahead and feel humiliated." She went on to say something that continues to resonate with me, "Go into battle dead already."

She told me about a Japanese swordsman who had written a book more than four hundred years ago, who had gone into battle dead already. At the time, he was the premier swordsman in Japan. He said the reason he was so good with his sword was because he had no hesitation during a battle, believing he was dead already. Killing that fear set him free.

To me, humiliation was death. If you acknowledge and

tell the truth that you've already been humiliated, you have nothing to lose. You're free to concentrate on the job at hand because you're not focused on the possible negative outcome.

I used to walk around performing all sorts of crazy, humiliating stunts, like dressing (or undressing in this case!) as a nudist for Halloween or playing a giant rapping lizard, thinking—even believing—that I understood what humiliation really meant.

I didn't.

When I was the butt of my own jokes, I was in control. But when the breakup of my marriage played out on TV, I had no control over people's reactions. And, to be certain, the situation was no laughing matter.

Even though the demise of my first marriage took place in front of millions of viewers, it ended up being something I had to go through because, in the end, it forced me to *see* the truth about people I once loved and allowed me to embrace them for who they are and more importantly, are not.

Dear Nanny-Cam,

Thanks!

Love,
Jenni

The night my husband told me our marriage was over, I thought my life was over, too. Everything I believed and lived for was gone—or so I thought. Almost everyone I knew was telling me I would know why I went through this, someday, and with time, things would get better. Although it was hard to understand or see, and to be certain, was really hard to hear in the moment, as time slowly passed, it began to make sense.

My public journey was the best thing that could have happened to me. Though I wish it could have stayed more private, perhaps the public humiliation was the great impetus for me to make some very necessary changes I wouldn't have otherwise made if I hadn't been on reality television. I can confess that however painful that period of time was, I wouldn't change a thing. It turns out my divorce from Chris was a loofah for my life.

I was scrubbed raw.

It was hell.

I survived.

And best of all, I learned that my failures do not define me.

Dear Failure,

I am writing this letter to offer my sincere thanks. I know in the beginning I really didn't like you at all. To be completely honest, I didn't find anything remotely attractive about you.

Sorry, harsh but true.

You were an annoyance and not a part of my life plan. As we spent more and more time together, I realized you have so many wonderful qualities and so much to offer. I think people misunderstand you. You always cared about what was best for my life and helped me become stronger. If I may offer a little constructive criticism, you can be severe and your timing is usually totally wrong, but we all have things to work on. Do you think we will always be good friends? I never thought I would say this but I hope so. Why? If it weren't for you, I would not have been led to the greatest joys in my life. So, until we hang again . . .

I love you,
Jenni

I wanted to learn to be truthful and authentically present for the people who loved me and whoever might be in my future. My marriage was over and I had to understand that was actually a new beginning. That's the pain and joy of being on your journey.

Without it ending I would have never been able to begin my life again. I desperately wanted a life that was full, one that I could share with someone who had their own responsibilities and who wasn't competing with me for the spotlight. I needed to be assured that I could feel loved, safe, secure, attractive, and desired. Through my many hours of therapy, speaking to my Spiritual Father, leaning on friends, and the passing of time that followed my divorce, I finally understood that I made mistakes in my relationship, ones I can now look back on and accept as my own. I felt like a complete failure when my marriage collapsed. I would have done anything to make it work.

When you go through a traumatic event such as a divorce or a death of a loved one, you will most likely discover who your real friends and allies are—and aren't. I vividly recall how my parents' friends took sides when my mom and dad split up. I watched people she loved dearly abandon her at her weakest. Naturally, I didn't think about the fallout from my split with Chris, but it came.

Though my immediate family was kind as my marriage crumbled, they could never seem to find the right words or the ability to nurture me through in a way that I found supportive. They liked Chris, but truth be told, my mother never wanted me to marry him in the first place. She never said the words, but I knew she was thinking when he left, *I told you so.* It would take her many years to confess this was how she really felt. When I asked her why she never said anything, she told me it was something I'd have to figure out for myself. In this case, her decision to not speak up was a form of tough love. And, she was right to stay quiet because there's no way I would have listened to what she would have said back then anyway.

I've found that when someone goes through loss, people often retreat because they don't know what to say or do, and maybe that's how our friends and family felt. It makes sense, but it doesn't make it any easier to accept.

Watching how everyone responded when my husband left me was an uncomfortable new beginning. Losing some longtime friends was almost as painful. My ah-ha moment that I had moved on came the day I realized I no longer missed Chris. I was sorry I had to go through the storm but it forced me to face my worst fears as they were all right in front of me.

There is great power in thinking through the things you really want. I spent too many years dwelling on what I couldn't have while making up every excuse I could think of to justify what was missing.

I took zero responsibility for my lack of action or participation in my own life. In the process, I discovered that I was the real roadblock stopping myself from achieving my dreams. It had nothing to do with my parents, my bosses, or my husband. It was me.

I prayed.

And I prayed—

And then I prayed some more . . . . *for guidance, wisdom, family, and a home.*

I allowed my faith to carry me through and bring me to a place where I could embrace that *over* and *beginning* really are the *same.* There is great power in change. Some people can only see change as scary, negative, and unwanted, but most often we find ourselves in a far better place we were in on the other side of that fear and resistance to a critical life adjustment. It doesn't matter if it's leaving an unfulfilling job, a miserable marriage, or moving to a new home. Change requires courage and strength to not only to make them but to also embrace them. As time went on, my prayers were being answered, as wisdom came first. It revealed so much to me, especially when it came to my ex and what I truly wanted in a relationship.

I didn't let a fair amount of time pass after my breakup with Chris before I wanted to get back into the world of dating. There was a hole in my life that I wanted to fill with someone, anyone, because I was lonely. When we first separated, I was full of angst and fear that I was too old to ever find someone new. To make matters worse, there were plenty of people in my life feeding my insecurities with comments they thought were funny, when in fact they were hurtful.

THINGS I DID *NOT* NEED TO HEAR

1. A woman in her late thirties has as much chance of finding a husband as being hit by a meteor.
2. Your clock has ticked. The eggs are dead. No children for you.
3. Just saw your ex-husband with a girl.
4. Just saw your ex-husband with a *cute* girl.
5. Just saw your ex-husband with a cute girl that looks *eighteen*.

I was hearing all of this and more. And hello, I don't know any woman who wants to hear any of that, especially when they are vulnerable. What I really needed was a mental makeover. But that would take time and I was too afraid of being alone to put off finding the love of my life for very long. I wasn't sure what was waiting for me out there: I often believed nothing was and was doing my best to convince myself that it would be okay if I ended up alone. Of course, it wasn't how I really felt.

For as far back as I can remember I have been afraid to sleep alone. I know it sounds odd but when I was younger, I had my mom lay in bed with me until I fell asleep. This went on well into grade school. All during college and even after college, I had roommates who shared a room with me. Then came my now ex-husband, so there was always someone else around. (*Note to Mom: if you are reading this we did *not* have sex before we were married, I promise.)

Call it fear of abandonment, insecurity, or simply an inability to cope with loneliness—whatever the reasons, I could not imagine living alone. Even after I split from Chris, it didn't take me very long to find someone else to live with. A girl roommate—a friend I didn't know very well—took me in because I didn't want to stay in the house I had shared with Chris. There was a lot of teasing from Jeff that I had suddenly become a U-Haul lesbian. I hadn't. But given what I'd been through, who would have blamed me if I suddenly decided to swim in the lady pond and kiss Katy Perry and like it?

My friend was very kind and extremely supportive at a time when I was weak and vulnerable. I was extremely appreciative for the time I lived with her. But it was time to put on my big-girl pants, move out, and be on my own. And I did!

My first night alone in my new house, I did what any other normal girl would do: I grabbed my two dogs, put them on the bed, and made my first attempt at sleeping alone. I could call it home—*my home.*

The first night, I felt a sense of bewilderment. *What do I do with myself? Which side should I sleep on? What pillows feel right and so on?* I tossed and turned until I finally got out of bed—trying to escape the discomfort of being by myself—and began pacing all around my house trying to think of something to do. (And cooking something was not an option, because I'd only have to cook for myself . . . because I was ALONE!) I could clean . . . Nah.

TV? No one to watch it with.

Reading was not an option because it involves being "interested" in things other than oneself—and at the time I wasn't interested in anyone but me.

Then, just when I thought I was on the verge of a mini-breakdown, I stopped and thought, *Maybe I should just . . .*

Be grateful.
Be content.
Be quiet.
Be thankful for this coherent moment of stillness.
Be thankful that Jeff Lewis does not know where I live.

It didn't take me long to realize that there are several fantastic benefits to sleeping alone: The TV can remain on all night; the extra leg space is awesome; there's no snoring, unless you count the sounds that sometimes come from my two dogs. For a while, I still slept crammed to one side of the bed, optimistic and hopeful that Prince Charming was coming. (And boy did he ever, in the form of a wonderful Greek-American Orthopedic Surgeon from Chicago . . . but more on him later.)

Long before I would meet my Prince Charming, let's be real, I had to kiss a lot of frogs. Whether you consider it a rite of passage or a means to an end, dating after a divorce can be brutal. To ease my way back into the game, I decided to seek the advice of a fellow Bravo reality star who makes a living coaching singles like me to find true love—Ms. Patti Stanger.

Once I came out of my post-divorce fog, I realized there was a close friend of mine who I found myself attracted to. We had a history of playful flirtation. On Valentine's Day, with both of us reeling from recent breakups, we met for dinner and drinks, which ended romantically, a bit of a surprise, albeit a pleasant one. Still, I was so new at dating I didn't know what to do. I didn't want to be too overbearing or aggressive so I asked Patti for help.

This was her advice: Write him a text that reads, "Valley girls are hot. You don't need your passport to come to this side of the hill. Your serve."

You see, I live in an area of Los Angeles known as the San Fernando Valley. In L.A., that has the potential to make me geographically undesirable for someone who lives on the west side of the city. I thought it was a risk, but Patti, being the expert at love, and me, being, well, not, I decided to push the send button. I'm baaaaaack!

I never heard back from the guy again.

Like, ever.

(I actually never say things like I did in that text. Like, ever.)

What I should have done was text him to say that someone took my phone and sent that message. But really, what was the point?

Even so, I have to admit, that text message was good for a lot of laughs, so it was worth it.

Sort of.

From that point on, I had a string of bad dates that have provided tremendous comic relief. I went into autopilot doing what a lot of divorcées do—I put myself out there and got back on the horse. My first real "date" was with a really hot guy. Stupid hot. I mean stupid and hot. On our date he launched into his thoughts on why he should try to become an actor. He genuinely believed he could do it. He suggested that I could start taking him to my auditions, or even put him on *Flipping Out*. It was right around the time that he ordered a random broth soup for dinner that I decided to end our date early. When your date orders soup for dinner, it's hard to case the menu for a real meal without feeling piggy. The next day, he asked if he could borrow my video camera. I didn't respond after that.

I was never sure if I was being asked out because I was on

television or for other reasons. Regardless, I started to under-stand how rich men feel when they wonder if a chick is dating them for their money or for them. It's not like I had a lot of money—I didn't—but it seemed like people were enamored with the idea of going out with someone who was on TV.

Then there was the guy who showed up at my house in the middle of summer in a long black trench coat, channeling his best Keanu Reeves look from *The Matrix*. There was yet another date who seemed so nice when he asked me to come see a "show" he was working on as a producer. I thought he was handsome and fun. After the final curtain fell, he came over to me and planted a full-on French kiss in front of a large crowd of people. I thought, *Wow, I never dreamed this would be my new life* as I sat stunned in the audience of *Dancing with the Stars*. Later that night we went for sushi. Somehow he got a sliver in his finger from his chopstick and he couldn't finish eating until someone from the kitchen helped him get the sliver out with tweezers. He left me sitting alone at the table for twenty minutes.

I mean, c'mon. I told him I didn't think we'd be having any more dates. A few days later, I received a letter from him saying he hoped I would find someone who I would want to be in the sandbox with. It was sweet. But I still never talked to him again.

I met one guy for a coffee date. By the time I arrived, he'd almost finished his coffee. I wasn't sure if I was supposed to get my own coffee or if he'd offer. He didn't. He then launched into a long discussion about his rehab and things he likes to do on dates, like chopping vegetables for salads and watching foreign movies. I thought coffee dates were supposed to be short, but two hours later, I was still listening to him "share." Truth be told, I didn't say much on that date, mostly because I couldn't get a word in edgewise. That relationship wasn't going to work out.

One time I gave my number to a guy after telling me he was leaving for Canada for a few weeks. He said he'd like to take me out when he got back. I thought he was really cute, so I let him put his number in my phone. For two weeks, he texted me the sweetest messages about how he couldn't wait to see me and how excited he was to go out on a date. I was on cloud nine. Finally someone was treating me nice! When he got back, we made a plan to meet. However, when he came to pick me up, I had no idea who the guy was standing at my front door. You see, I had his friend put his number in my phone, too, and I'd forgotten which guy I was communicating with. Worse, he was barely twenty-one years old—though I think he might have been eighteen with a fake ID. We went out that night but it was, shall we say, awkward, especially when he said I reminded him of his mother.

And then . . . there was *Huggles*.

Huggles and I went on thirteen dates that always ended in a hug. It wasn't like I wanted to jump his bones, but seriously, hugs? It made it hard to tell if he was into me or not. I had planned to break up at dinner on that thirteenth date, but Huggles started talking first. He blurted out that he had cancer and was finally through his treatments.

When I told Jeff, he said, "How can you break up with him now?"

Jeff had a point, so I went on seven more dates that ended in seven more hugs. It wasn't working for me, cancer or no cancer. There would be no more giving snuggles for Huggles.

After Huggles, I had a hot encounter with an actor.

Okay, wait.

Not *that* kind of hot encounter.

It was more of a *heated* exchange. We were working in a gyro booth at a church fund-raiser. The guy and I started talking and after a bit I said, "What do you do?"

He said, "I'm an actor."

(We were in L.A. Of course he was.)

Then he actually pulled out his cell phone that had his demo reel all cued up and said "Here's my work. That's me on *Drew Carey, General Hospital, Jimmy Kimmel*—I'm a huge celebrity in Cyprus and I'm even bigger in Romania."

"Oh, great, I'll be right back." I wanted to get away as fast as I could. Been there, done that, and have divorce papers to prove it.

Just then someone came up to me and said, "You're Jenni from *Flipping Out*! I love your show. Can we get a picture?"

"Sure," I said.

Afterward, the guy turned to me and said, "Oh, it looks like someone else is a big celebrity, too."

Yuck! I almost contemplated changing professions . . . well . . . for about sixty seconds. That's how that exchange made me feel.

Why?

Because I used to be just like that guy, trying to prove to anyone who would listen that I was a bigger deal or more successful then I actually was. I took it as a wonderful sign that this happened at a church festival. God, I prayed, someday I might be at a church with a man I loved who wanted to share his life with me and not just his résumé.

7

Navigating Around Negativity

> Don't let your past hold your future hostage. And
> don't let the old stale opinions of others affect your
> fresh current dreams.
>
> —LL COOL J, RAPPER

I was standing in line at the Coffee Bean and Tea Leaf in West Hollywood one morning when a very well-dressed man came over to me and said, "Excuse me . . . I have met all of the greats, from Lucille Ball to Sylvester Stallone, and I wanted to say hello because you are one of the few people in this town I have always wanted to meet."

"Really? You know I'm not Elaine from *Seinfeld*, right?" I said, in a tone filled with utter shock and disbelief.

The man whipped out his phone to call his wife. When she answered, he handed me the phone.

"My husband and I just love you. We admire how you handle Jeff and everything with so much patience. . . ."

Anyone who knows me will tell you that patience has never been my strong suit. So for a girl bent on improvement, this chance meeting made me feel like I must be finally doing something right. Leaving the Coffee Bean floating on air, I made my way across town to meet a potential agent at one of the biggest talent agencies in Hollywood. I felt like this would be my lucky day.

I checked in with the receptionist and was asked to take a seat in the lobby. Just as I sat down, a beautiful young starlet walked in who wasn't currently working on anything that I was aware of. She got shuttled right through the lobby with several agents all over her. It was hard not to notice the difference in our reception.

I waited.

Thirty minutes passed.

Forty-five minutes.

Fifty minutes later they called me in.

I won't lie.

I was pissed.

I was in the agent's office for a couple of minutes before he looked up and said, "You are talented but you have a very long way to go. Good luck with your show."

That's it?

That's all he had to say?

Let me get this straight. A nonworking actress walks in minutes after I do, is fawned over, and me, the one with the hit show on Bravo gets the brush-off?

Okay, to be fair, in retrospect, what he said wasn't wrong. In fact, he was right on the money—I just wasn't ready to hear what he had to say. His delivery stung and the information was devastating. He certainly didn't need to call me into his office to break *that* news to me. A phone call would have sufficed. By this point however, I had gotten used to this message, which wasn't helping matters. When someone in a position of authority or power spoke, I listened. It didn't matter if it was my mom, my acting teachers, casting agents, or even my employers. If they said I was no good, I embraced that notion. If they thought I was in over my head, I began to doubt myself. I remember once being told by someone on my soon to be dissolved business team that I should wear a fat suit to auditions to get parts. They thought I wasn't attractive enough to be the "hottie," so the job that was next in line was typically the bulky best buddy.

And if people underestimated my abilities, I lived down to their expectations instead of up to my own. Worse, I created excuse after excuse to support their influence over my own self-belief. Before I knew it, their opinions had a much higher value than mine. I adjusted my behavior to achieve those disappointing outcomes.

For most of us, there was once a time where we believed that anything was possible. As kids, our vision for the future was limitless—we could be whatever we dreamed. We could become a princess, a star basketball player, a veterinarian, or anything else our imaginations allowed us to see. Sadly, somewhere along the way, that fearlessness to dare and willingness to change the world can be taken over by other people telling us what is or isn't in our best interest.

At different points in our lives, we encounter the naysayer, skeptic, critic, the person who is full of negativity and somehow manages to suck out all of the fresh hope and energy from our dreams. Some people do tell us things we need to hear for our own good, yet others say things because it makes them feel better about themselves or their miserable, unsatisfying lives. Still others try to hold you back because they fear you might actually fulfill your dream and in the process, make them question their own choices in life. Finally, there are those people in the world that no matter how good things are, they have a special talent at only seeing the negative side of life. They are negative minded by nature—and will likely never change.

Like it or not, there are people in this world who prefer to see you messed up rather than happy. Take it from me—these are the people who thrive on your misery and will do anything they can to perpetuate that negative environment as a way of staying in control and not facing their own life lessons. They'll say things like, "You used to be crazy and funny. What happened?," or "I liked you much better when you weren't so calm. Are you okay?"

Although it might be hard not to take negative comments personally, you have to remember that most of the time, their criticism isn't about you—it's about them. Perhaps they've been making excuses about why they aren't succeeding at the things they want to do and are turning those statements into advice for you. "You're too old, everyone will make fun of you, what will your mother think?" are all statements designed to make you doubt and fear that whatever it is you're trying to do simply won't work.

I'm not saying that everyone is a critic. There are some people who will genuinely be interested in what you want to do and will help you try to figure out the best way to achieve that goal. If you have that kind of support in your life, that's awesome. The likelihood, however, is that within the circle of people in your life there may be naysayers secretly disguised as friends and loved ones who may be out to prove why you'll fail, before you even get started. They want, *they need*, you to stay exactly where you are—your place in life is comfortable and nonthreatening to *them* . . . they don't want to lose that! It's like the husband who watches his wife lose a bunch of weight and then brings home pie, cake, and ice cream all the time. Seeing his wife get into shape forces him to realize how out of shape he's become. It makes him uncomfortable to see his bride take control of her health and well-being.

There are a lot of people out there in the world who fall back on being a total downer without knowing they're doing it. It's an automatic response that they're not even conscious of. When in doubt, learn to ignore the naysayers, critics, and skeptics and carry on! Navigating around and through the negativity you can encounter requires clarity, discipline, and practice. You can learn to do it.

In our office, there is sometimes a disconnect between what

Jeff finds appropriate in the workplace and what everyone else expects. In addition, it has been hard for us to set boundaries between Jeff's personal space and the workspace. This is a challenge for anyone who chooses to operate a business out of their home. I think Jeff operates this way partly for convenience and also to keep things exactly the way he wants them. And that extends, as fans of the show know, to his lunch.

> No onions, no onions, no onions!
>
> —JEFF LEWIS

I would say that Jeff has major OCD, and has a need to be in control, even of the tiniest details. He even has instilled a strict set of rules for everyone to follow that includes no number two in his bathrooms. If you really have to go, you can count on being terrorized for many months. Bring out the lie detector, I haven't gone number two in Jeff's office in twelve years. There is also a limit of sixty seconds during bathroom breaks. If you exceed that limit, Jeff will scream, "What are you doing in there? You better not be going number two!" When you don't use the full sixty seconds, you actually get rollover minutes. (I have acquired a plethora of rollover minutes over the years.)

As a reward for my respectful bathroom behavior, I am trusted by Jeff to tell employees and contractors the following: "If you sprinkle when you tinkle, be a sweetie and wipe the seatie."

These types of exchanges happen all of the time in our office. The key to surviving at Jeff Lewis Design is to abide by his set of rules.

When you sense disapproval from your boss at work, it's extremely important to distinguish between constructive and destructive criticism. It's not any easier to be the boss than it is to be the employee. It would be ideal if everyone understood there are different sets of responsibilities that make each position unique and necessary. For example, there is a lot of micromanaging in the construction and renovation world. We are constantly making phone calls to ensure that the workers show up and meet deadlines. Delays will not only cause your budget to skyrocket but also add tremendous pressure to an already stressful situation. You have to be incredibly aggressive and demanding to complete a project on time and on budget.

It is easy to see someone with this mind-set as being difficult and uncompromising, but it is necessary to get the job done.

I better understood what it's like to be the boss when Jeff was out sick for the day with food poisoning. It certainly was an eye-opening experience because I hadn't ever put myself in his shoes before. For the first time, I had an assistant who wasn't moving fast enough and anticipating what I needed. I found myself getting barky and short-tempered. I also realized there were other people in the office looking at me, judging how I was acting. In a single day, I'd become a total bosshole.

Oh.

Right.

This must be what Jeff feels like when I am not on my "A" game.

To feel valued, to know, even if only once in a while, that you can do a job well is an absolutely marvelous feeling.

—BARBARA WALTERS

There have been many times I witnessed Jeff get angry with me or someone else for not doing their job. It's a simple enough request, and after spending a day being Jeff, I had a much clearer understanding of why he gets so upset. Since Jeff can't let mistakes slide by without some type of response, we have made a game out of errors in our office. Let's say you make a mistake like accidentally taking home Jeff's credit card or his keys. As punishment, you have to wear an XXL white one-piece painter's jumpsuit, which makes everyone look like the Stay Puft Marshmallow Man! Of course, my way to cope with having to wear the "suit of shame" is to accessorize, accessorize, accessorize. (A girl can never go wrong with a beaded necklace and a set of bangles!)

On one occasion, after committing an office crime, Jeff made me wear the suit to a meeting with a group of executives from Dunn-Edwards, the company Jeff has a paint line with. Instead of causing me great embarrassment, it made them smile, which meant I took a potentially combative situation and turned it into something exciting and fun. Wearing this outfit was meant to be a punishment and ended up supporting the company. By the end of our meeting, I told Jeff that we should make fashionable smocks and painter's suits as a side business. Now *that's* what I call going toward the hit!

I sometimes think of Jeff's OCD as Occasionally Causing Disturbances. To see the smile on Jeff's face when he has scared someone to the point of heart failure, you know this man has the heart of a child. This may be something that has linked us together all of these years.

Are there times at work that we have fun and mess around?

You bet!

At times, we're unprofessional.

And to be certain, there are lots of circumstances where we butt heads. It's important to remember that work relationships are relationships that involve human beings, with emotions, frailties, and quirks. As a professional assistant, I realize that sometimes my job is to be a sounding board. It comes with the territory. But, it doesn't mean you have to let your boss break you down and take your identity or sense of self-worth. Don't be so desperate for their approval in the first place. Just do your job, and do it well. It makes it harder to get reprimanded if you're doing what you're supposed to do in the first place.

I was curious about the true definition of the word *boss*, so I looked it up in the dictionary. Here is what I found:

> boss: *noun*
> - A person in charge of a worker or organization
> - A round knob, stud, or other protuberance in particular
> - A cow

Some people only know how to manage through creating fear. They yell, scream, throw tantrums, and bully their way through every situation. They use negative language to get what they want—whether it's the meeting of a deadline or the completion of a task they didn't think was possible. Most people can't handle being the target of negative language, so they freeze or, worse, completely shut down. When that happens, nothing gets done and no one can excel. The solution is simple: Address the problem and get rid of the fear. Focus on the job that needs to get done and just do it. That will usually mitigate the bullying. Don't feed the monster by getting defensive, trying to prove you're worthy and they're wrong. If you do, they'll always be able to keep you in that place of fear, believing you're horrible at your job and can't do anything right.

"You're right, I did that," is often a great place to start. Own it. They'll have no place left to go with their anger because you aren't throwing gasoline on the fire defending yourself. And if all else fails, make 'em laugh! Whenever possible, I try to deal with these types of people with humor because it's a great diffuser. Even if I have to be the butt of a joke to break the tension, I'll take that hit if it means moving forward. It relives the pressure and helps to put everyone back on track.

Jeff often finds it funny to ride me about my fashion sense, especially when it comes to what I wear to work. We all know he's a true fashion plate, with his Mr. Rogers–inspired style, mom jeans, turned-up collars on his rotating assortment of Lacoste short-sleeve shirts, and rainbow-colored selection of Converse sneakers. It's hard to compete with that, but I do my best to counter his *GQ*-ness with my Dora the Explorer style, or a *too-tight* jumpsuit that is too tight (which I deliberately wore to annoy Jeff because I'm pretty sure he could see my ovaries through it), or my salute to Korean fashion with a pant/skirt that had a crotch that came down to my knees (which drove Jeff crazy). I select my outfits based on how they make me feel or how entertaining they might be (and perhaps, at times, merely to get revenge . . .)

I spend a lot of time on job sites where sneakers and cargo pants are a more appropriate choice for my work wardrobe than say, a dress and heels. I have endured a contractor or *ten* looking up my skirt. I will admit that sometimes it is better to be in the right gear on the construction site. However, I like to get dressed up for work, especially when I know we'll be seeing clients. Without fail, whenever I wear a skirt and high heels, Jeff makes me go up a ladder, on a roof, or down into an unfinished basement that's still dirt or mud. It's at these times Jeff's familiar scowl breaks into a naughty little kid smile. He's a grown-up man with a heart of a child.

I always try to make the job fun and find the joy, especially when the pressure is on. Conversely, I've noticed in certain professional settings, people will pit one person against another as a method of creating negative competition instead of cooperation. They invent a dust storm that makes everyone defensive and tense. Reigning through creative confusion is a way for this type of person to control a situation. Every day will bring unexpected turns to the left and then sudden ones to the right. OH MY GOD! How can we navigate a path through our workday that is sporadic and unpredictable?

Find a way!

Dealing with office politics is a lot like the shows *Survivor* or *Big Brother*: People make alliances to survive, and sometimes win. Even in a small office like ours, alliances are made! Alliances are caused by mutual self-interests. They're about personal advancement or holding someone else back because they are threatened by their existence. It doesn't really matter if you're working at a large company or in someone's living room, office politics are a no-win proposition. If you focus on creating or maintaining alliances to protect yourself as opposed to assisting your boss and doing your work, then you are absolutely misdirected. Steer clear of all the basic nonsense that doesn't do anything but slow down your day and create more problems. Just do your job.

Things have a way of working out. I have done my fair share of stirring things up and then spent way too much time worrying about it for weeks at a time. It's especially tricky when you are friends or social with your boss and/or co-workers because there is a very thin line between the personal and professional rapport. Never forget that any time you are out with people you work with, even if it is after hours, they are watching you. It helps to see gossip as a critic.

All gossip does is stir up panic. If you're spending time around the water cooler, or on Facebook and Twitter gossiping about your co-workers, your teammates, it's a sure sign that you are not at your desk doing your job. Who wants to spend their day looking over their shoulder, worrying if their job is somehow being compromised by someone else's doubt or insecurities? Keeping your mouth shut and your eyes open takes discipline and practice.

If I so much as look at Jeff while he is badgering me on something, he's got me. He wins. That's when I go back to my to-do list and just do the work. It doesn't matter to me that Jeff still asks me to get his 140-degree latte or replenish the mints in his tin that he keeps in his glove compartment. My own family's business taught me that it's everyone's job to do whatever it takes to make the business work.

I am by no means a "yes" man employee, one who tells Jeff what he wants to hear instead of what he needs to hear. I have stood up to Jeff in certain situations, even if he doesn't like what I have to say. If he is doing something that is out of line, I tell him so, whether it's his behavior with me or someone else. Of course that can be scary, because what I say may be perceived as being inappropriate, which places me on the receiving end of a major personality eruption. Jeff does get mad at me, but at some point, twenty minutes or two days later, he sees that my speaking out was simply to get something done. I know he respects me for having the courage to step out of my comfort zone from time to time, even if it puts me in the line of fire. The key is to protect your boss and the business. They may not say it, but I am sure they will appreciate this about you.

TEN CAN'TS TO HELP YOU GET CANNED!

1. Can't stop being an independent thinker
2. Can't understand whatever your title is . . . it's spelled S-E-R-V-A-N-T
3. Can't perform because you feel underpaid
4. Can't stop pouting because you don't receive "positive reinforcement"
5. Can't stop expecting premium health insurance
6. Can't quit mirroring your boss if he is grumpy, defensive, or sarcastic
7. Can't stop repeating "I'm entitled"
8. Can't stop throwing co-workers under the bus to impress your boss
9. Can't stop oversharing personal or business information
10. Can't stop telling your boss this job is only a "pit stop"

8

Work, Don't Worry!

> Nothing will work unless you do.
>
> —MAYA ANGELOU

My mom has always been a major worrier, which is why I am one, too. To be honest, I think this is a common trait amongst us Greeks. Her day-to-day existence seemed to be an endless cycle of cooking, worrying, cleaning, and worrying some more. This explains how my worrying blossomed into a full-blown epidemic. I became an expert at building up tremendous amounts of paranoia. When my dogs would be sick, for instance, I would fear the worst—a parasite!—when usually the problem could be solved with the smallest spoonful of Pepto-Bismol. Most of the time, 90 percent of whatever I worried about never came true. But what did come true were ulcers and acid reflux. Even though I knew this, I'd still find a way to spin things around in my head, feeding the negativity. I finally realized what this kind of worrying was doing to me. I had to stop and ask why I was putting myself through this in the first place? I was Chicken Little and the sky was always falling.

Believe it or not, it wasn't until I began working with Jeff that I discovered what the true meaning of hard work and dedication were really all about. For the most part, he doesn't worry about it, he just does it. Jeff works amazingly hard and spends his time pursuing the things he wants to achieve. The reason for his success is because he works at it. I am inspired by his drive, passion, and to-do lists. He gets an awesome amount accomplished in a day.

After surviving the massive humiliation of being dumped on national television, people around me began noticing a change. When I finally realized that all the time I'd spent complaining over the years could have been used working toward my goals, I kind of wished for that time back.

God has a mysterious way of giving us what we need when we need it. Sadly, the circumstances that I would face next would show me once and for all that there's a great big world out there. I was newly single and living on my own when my sister Krisann was diagnosed with stage 3 breast cancer. Her prognosis wasn't good. She had to have seventeen lymph nodes removed and undergo intensive chemotherapy and radiation treatments. I could see the impact my sister's illness was having on our mother, who mostly suffered in silence as she tried to appear strong. I could also see the toll it was taking on Krisann's husband, who despite being a wonderful physician couldn't do anything to help his wife get better.

Krisann's radiation therapy was going to take place in Los Angeles. Since she lives in Palm Springs, she stayed with me during the week while going through treatment and with her family on the weekends. At first, seeing her in pain was hard for me to deal with. I was still so wrapped up in my own pain and suffering that I wasn't dialed into hers. I focused on "being busy" to escape the pain of watching my sister suffer. Despite her illness, she was supportive and cared about what was going on in my life. I was selfish, self-absorbed, and wasn't the support she needed. I look back on my behavior and can share that it taught me the true meaning of recognizing what is really important.

I watched my sister face her biggest fear: getting cancer. She had worried for years that she would get sick and that worry turned into a reality. The day that she embraced that she may die I believe her life changed forever. She buried worry and in turn worry did not bury her.

When Krisann first got sick, I could see the dramatic impact it had on all of her children, but it was especially hard on her youngest boy, Christian. The day my sister had her first surgery, I picked him up from school. He was angry, terrified, and confused. I did what I could to offer him comfort, but at the time I couldn't offer Christian what he needed the most—to be with his mom. It was a really difficult time for him. To cope, he channeled his emotions into learning to play the piano all on his own. We discovered he was blessed with a God-given gift—a talent he might never have known had his mom not gotten sick.

After Krisann was diagnosed, the one thing that kept her going was wanting to be there for her children. I have a tremendous amount of respect for my sister and brother-in-law—their commitment and dedication to their three boys is inspiring. Their son Nicholas, then fifteen, has special needs. He has a brain tumor, suffers from multiple seizures daily, and has autistic characteristics. Now eighteen, Nicholas can't really communicate but goes to school and engages in multiple activities. He has touched so many lives around him, and despite his challenges and daily pain, he is a remarkably happy and optimistic young man.

We knew the one thing that devastated Krisann while going through chemo was losing her hair from the treatments. Growing up, I was blessed with a frizzy, unmanageable mop while my sister had a beautiful head of flowing hair. Coming together as a family meant we could face whatever obstacles life threw our way. We decided to take pictures of every family member, including my two dogs, wearing horrible wigs, which provided much-needed laughter. My family's shared faith allowed this silliness to be an option at an unbelievably difficult time.

During her treatment, I had to go to New York to shoot

promos for Bravo's "Summer by Bravo" campaign. (There are many members of the "Bravo Circus" who convene under one roof for these campaigns, led by our fearless ringmaster Andy Cohen. Jeff has been soaked year after year—a prank that never gets old.) Over the years I have become friendly with many under the Bravo Big Top, one of whom is Tabatha Coffey, hair genius and star of *Tabatha Takes Over*. During the filming of the summer campaign I had a scene with her where we were fencing and she cut my hair with her sword into a beautiful shoulder bob. I mentioned that my sister had lost her hair in her battle with cancer and she had a hard time finding a wig that looked and felt real.

I was stunned when two days later a wig from Tabatha appeared at my sister's front door. Krisann's spirit was lifted by this incredibly kind gesture. I later learned that Tabatha lost her mother to cancer a few weeks after we were filming in New York. And it blew me away, how some people move through the world thinking about others despite their personal pain. I wanted to be someone who genuinely cared about others and showed it—someone who made good things happen for other people.

I got the opportunity to do this when I met Abbey Curran at the Inspirational Women of the Year Awards sponsored by Susan G. Komen. Abbey was receiving an award for her service. This firecracker of a young woman won the title of Miss Iowa USA 2008 despite her cerebral palsy. For the last ten years she has built the Miss You Can Do It Pageant for girls ages 4–24 with disabilities. What ignited my spirit about this event was how each and every one of these girls, despite their severe disabilities, did not embrace defeat. They exuded joy. Pure joy. Had they been teased and told the BIG 3 (Not Good Enough)? It is safe to say every single day. Were the odds against them? And then some! Were they told they could never have the desires of their heart? In stereo!

Yet each and every one of them—despite their limitations—were happy. They were pursuing their dreams, with hope and determination, of changing the world.

I realized, yet again, this is what we all should strive for in life.

It was a necessary reminder that even though there is always going to be some kind of challenge, we can do anything if we put our mind to it. I fought against that for so many years when I should have embraced it.

Instead of wondering, "Why me?" it was time to shift that attitude to "Why *not* me?"

Studies have shown that from the time we are born until we are eighteen years old we are told, "No, don't, stop, quit and you're going to fail" 180,000 times! I hate to brag but I am sure I have logged in over a million.

It took me a long time to understand that my pain and insecurities did not have to define my thinking process. Look at all of the people out there in the world who have problems and are living life to the fullest anyway. I wanted to become one of *those* people—but I didn't have a clue as to how to get started. I needed to take responsibility for my life once and for all!

Many times over the years, Kathleen told me to "work, don't worry" and that I was "always throwing the baby out with the bathwater." I never really understood what that meant, so I looked it up. The expression *"implies that an entire idea, concept, practice, or project doesn't need to be rejected or discontinued if part of it is good. The baby, in this sense, represents the good part that can be preserved. The bathwater, on the other hand, usually is dirty after the baby is washed and needs to be discarded, just like the parts of the concept that are bad or useless."* I was throwing everything out when things weren't going the way I wanted.

Putting together my *Old School Kids Beats* CD had become a passion project that most everyone around me told me I shouldn't do. There were lots of people saying it was a terrible idea. They warned me that if I followed through with the project, I'd never be taken seriously in the business as a rapper or an actor ever again. Jeff told me if I released the CD, he thought it would be a passport for me to replace one of the Wiggles, because he heard there was an opening in the group.

For as long as I have been rapping, I have received lots of criticism for my love of rhyming and fresh beats. No one could understand what my attraction was, especially to old-school rap. I grew up listening to Will Smith, LL Cool J, Young MC, Digital Underground, and many others who influenced me from the moment I heard them.

If you're a fan of *Watch What Happens Live,* Kathleen and I cowrote the theme song for Andy Cohen's very popular television show. Word up, homie. That's me on your TV when you hear, "Andy Cohen's got the 411 . . ."

The first time I realized the song had gone viral was after I landed in Burbank and a couple of people on the plane turned on their phones (one was a man in a business suit). I did a double take when I heard their ringtones were "Andy Cohen's got the 411 . . ." It got so popular that Hoda Kotb sang it when Andy appeared on her and Kathy Lee's show. The entire audience chanted the song when WWHL taped at South by Southwest Film Festival. It has even been played by the Tonight Show Band. Some of the biggest beat artists and songwriters in the business approached Andy to redo his theme song after his show took off, but he said "no way." He was loyal to our song and I am forever grateful and appreciative for his support.

What you say and the words you speak have a profound and powerful impact on the outcome of anything you attempt to do. My *Old School Kids Beats* CD was released in 2013. It was purchased by Toys R Us and was on sale nationwide in November 2013. I believed in the album. No matter how many times someone told me what a crazy, stupid, awful idea it was, I just smiled and said, "I don't agree" or nothing at all. This kind of strong will and perseverance didn't just happen overnight. It took some undoing and reprogramming of the way I approached everything in my life.

When I shot my first television commercial for Secret antiperspirant, the campaign's theme was "Outlast." The deodorant certainly does and for the first time I felt I could too.

My first Secret commercial was unlike anything I have ever done. The stunt work was challenging and the shoot took *thirty hours.* Whenever my energy would start to fade, Kathleen, who was on set, fed me small pieces of bacon. It was like she had a pocket full of tiny dog treats for me that kept me going. She whispered in my ear, "Hey, it works at the Westminster Dog Show!"

For much of the shoot, I was strung up in wires suspended from the ceiling. When I shot the scene that had me coming off a revolving dry cleaning rack to meet the man of my dreams on the top of a building, it took several tries before we got it right. On the second take, I fell flat on my face. I won't lie. It hurt. I got a little too much momentum and *smack!* I hit the floor. Every actor on the roof of the building was still posing in character, as if nothing had happened. Did they not see the flying Greek girl blow past them and ram her head into the ground? Thankfully, I was not hurt. In a strange way, while lying on the floor, I finally felt like I had certainly come a long way from Captain Coconut. I left the shoot black and blue from head to toe, covered my body in Icy Hot, and thought, *My dreams are finally coming true!*

Aside from airing the commercial on national television, the campaign was set to be a giant presence through the Internet and social media outlets. I was given two hand puppets requiring different voices and seven different scripts to memorize for the shoot. I was in the middle of finishing up filming for the sixth season of *Flipping Out,* and was exhausted but still had to stay focused, present, and bring my A game.

A lot of people walk through life half checked out. They walk down the street, texting, listening to music, doing their own thing, tuning out the world along the way. It takes an effort to be fully present—at work, at home, in your relationships, and with yourself. Just showing up is not enough. When you are fully engaged, the end product is always better because you are giving all of yourself instead of merely some. This is what I had to do while working on the Secret ad campaign. I was finally embracing the work and not the worry.

This realization had a profound impact on every area of my life. For example, when I am at work, I am now 100 percent committed to being present—I am dialed in to the business side of things in ways I could not have been while my attention was diverted. There were a lot of years when Jeff accused me of not being present, of being somewhere other than fully focused on his business.

If I'm the Better Player, Why Can't I Win? is a book written by Allen Fox, who was the tennis coach at Pepperdine University. It is about mind-set and the psychology of competition. It took me three years to finish the book—not that it wasn't interesting, I just wasn't interested. What I discovered, though, is what people are conditioned to focus on is extremely important. If you go into a performance with a fo-cus on the outcome, winning, losing, making a mistake, what's at stake, you inevitably set yourself up for failure. Your focus and concentration is on the wrong thing, which can make you nervous, uptight, and unable to perform at your peak. To be consistently at your best, you have to be in the moment—every moment. As a competitive tennis player, I totally understand that if I allow myself to get upset over losing a single point, I will lose the match. The second I allow my thoughts to get preoccupied with the win or loss of the match, I am no longer in the game. My attention is diverted and the likelihood that I can regain my focus is very low. Tennis is a mental game, one which is not just based on skill but also mental rigor. The book helped me understand that I had been my own worst enemy on and off the court.

My never-ending pursuit of perfectionism was a no-win battle for everyone involved, especially for me because I wasn't doing the work needed to achieve my goals and worse, creating excuses for why I couldn't without ever trying. It took time, but I finally admitted there is no such thing as *perfect*. There is no *perfect* job, no *perfect* partner, no *perfect* boss and no *perfect* me (or you, for that matter!). We are all works in progress.

Case in point: The Bravo A-list Awards helped me throw my focus on perfection out the window. Jeff and I were pre-senting and I bought an expensive designer gown that had to be altered. When I was packing, I discovered a hole in the

Jenni Pulos

delicate fabric of the dress. Up until that point, I would have let that little hole have the power to ruin my entire evening. Despite this, I decided that nobody would know the hole was even there. The night was the best of Bravo and I was happily present, flaws and all.

These days I approach everything I do with an appreciation that things happen. When you are so consumed with the perfect outcome you can't be present in the process. Learning to let go of my need to be perfect set me free—like an athlete who can work through the pain wall. Runners sometimes hit these during long races. They train themselves to work through the pain and keep running. I finally learned to work through my pain wall of perfection.

Excellence I can reach for. Perfection is God's business.

—MICHAEL J. FOX

If you were lucky enough to grow up feeling loved, worthy, supported, and good about yourself, then you will believe that is who you really are.

If, however, you grew up being told you aren't good enough, smart enough, pretty enough, talented enough, that you'd never amount to anything, then you will believe that is who you really are. It is almost as simple as computer in, computer out.

My mother never said negative things to me in a direct

way. They always came in the form of love-filled mixed messages, like, "When did your ankles get so fat?"; "Are you sure you want another helping of mashed potatoes?"; or "Why can't you find a job I can be proud of?" She was never trying to be mean. It was just her way of communicating.

It's important to understand that your acceptance of negative images of yourself doesn't make them true. Henry Ford once said, "Whether you think you can or you can't, you're right."

One theory to discontinue negative thoughts is to cancel them out as soon as they enter your brain. In fact, someone taught me that when negative thoughts or self-beliefs rear their ugly head, simply say "Cancel, Cancel" out loud. This simple action could take away any power that negative thought has over you. It also allows you the chance to take a step back from your negative talk and consciously learn a language that focuses on the positive. It's not easy to become an observer to your thoughts, but it's far better than drowning in them, if they're negative. Take it from me, I know!

Want to get a glimpse at what your life looks like to others? Get on a reality show and put it all out there for the world to see, judge, mock, and adore. Believe me, you'll want to change the channel . . . forever. The television that had been my babysitter turned into a truth-telling therapist.

There were so many times I watched *Flipping Out* and felt as though it was like one giant wake-up call. I could see what everyone else watching the show saw—a woman who appeared to have it all together on the outside. I had to learn what it meant to be authentic and fast. Only W-O-R-K was going to make this happen.

W—Willing
O—Organized
R—Ready
K—Keep the "can't" out of the mix

Once I began learning a new positive emotional language, my work and my life got a lot more interesting and fulfilling.

9

Top 10 Surefire Ways to Fail

> I have not failed. I've just found 10,000 ways that won't work!
>
> —THOMAS EDISON

What's the most dreaded F-word in the world?

In business and in life, I think it's *failure*.

I can pretty much confess that I've done *everything* wrong along the way. I've only gotten through it all by kicking and screaming, believing I was right. Boy, was I wrong!

I failed at marriage after two separations with the same guy and I thought we were happy!

I failed in my career. I wanted to become an actress but instead, I ended up starring in a reality television show about my day job, which I hoped no one in Hollywood would know about. My mom reminds me every chance she gets that I have spent the last seventeen years with my best work "on the cutting room floor." When I finally did get a show on TV, she said, "Your breasts look bulky!"

I failed at keeping my car and apartment clean.

I failed Spanish at UCLA.

And even *Flipping Out* has been something of a failure because my boss, Jeff Lewis, constantly reminds me how badly I screw things up.

Many of us hold onto the idea that failure is a negative experience that should be avoided at all costs. Sure, failure can be frustrating, maddening, hurtful, and even depressing, but it can also be a positive experience to learn and grow from. Fearing failure makes us less likely to take risks, which can lead us to success.

The more mistakes I made, the more I realized there was nothing to fear and only positive experiences to be gained. The trick to gaining something positive from failure is to find the reason why you've failed, learn from it, and then eliminate one or even twenty more things that have been obstacles. Look at failure as a teacher rather than something that defines you negatively.

When you fail, take a few minutes to think about what happened and why. And then ask yourself what you learned from the experience. There's always something good that comes out of trying and failing.

The most successful people I know, respect, and admire all have war stories and major battle scars from their failures. I know you've heard this before, but it's true: It doesn't matter how many times you fall down. It only matters that you get back up.

Here are a few interesting failures for you to consider:

- Michael Jordan was cut from his high school basketball team, missed more than 9,000 shots in his career, lost almost 300 games, and missed the game-winning shot twenty six times.
- Thomas Edison invented the perpetual cigar and cement furniture before coming up with the lightbulb.
- Albert Einstein's parents were told he might be mentally retarded.
- Elvis Presley didn't make the glee club at his school.
- The Beatles were turned down by Decca Records.
- Steven Spielberg dropped out of high school so he could concentrate on shooting movies.
- Babe Ruth struck out a record breaking 1,330 times before he became the home-run king.
- John Grisham's first book was rejected by sixteen agents and a dozen publishers. He actually sold his first book out of the trunk of his car.
- And finally, the average entrepreneur fails 3.8 times before succeeding.

Hey, David Letterman, did you know I applied in college to be an intern for your summer program and was rejected? Here is my Top Ten list:

My Top Ten Surefire Ways to Fail!

1. Don't do the work.

From the outside, show business may appear to be all glitz and glam, but like any job, it's still work. There were many times I'd try to "wing" a pitch for a new show or an audition and I wasn't prepared. I thought I could skate on my "natural" talent. For years, I'd roll into an audition, expecting applause and an occasional "nice job"—any type of feedback to make me feel validated. The result was usually a "don't call us, we *won't* call you" response and me missing out on a perfectly good opportunity. Like most everything in life, you get out what you put in. If you're truly interested in what you're doing, it will show in the results. It doesn't matter if you're folding sweaters at the Gap or serving cocktails at your local pub, there's a skill and a disciplined attitude required to make the most out of what you're doing. Here's what I know for sure: no one really sustains a career by being lucky. Robin Williams and Jim Carrey have often spoken about how they used to practice their material in the mirror for hours, days, weeks, and months—however long it took until it no longer felt rehearsed but natural. Succeeding requires dedication to your craft, continuing study, and learning to produce good work under difficult circumstances. That is when you have real value. The go-to person is the one who has done the work.

2. Don't keep your promises.

Has there ever been a time in your life when you knew you needed to take action, to do something, but you simply didn't follow through? We all fall victim to this—we make a promise with good intentions and somehow we allow it to fall into the abyss of our busy lives. A lot of times, a promise is made in a moment of goodwill. But what happens when that promise is broken?

In my case, I often over-promised and under-delivered, saying I'd read a script, researched an article, bought a book, or watched a film to learn more about a character I was preparing for, but I'd actually not done it. I'd come up with every excuse I could think of to avoid doing the work (see #1).

Guess what? You waste people's precious time and you can wreck relationships.

Making a promise isn't worth a thing if you aren't willing to follow through. In your business or personal life this is an act of destruction. You can't pledge to donate money to a charity and never write the check. Not keeping your promises is a surefire path to failure.

3. Keep lying because everyone is doing it.

When I was growing up, I often heard statements like, "Go ahead and try it, all of the cool kids are doing it. . . ." It didn't really matter what "it" was. From cigarettes to drinking, if the cool kids were doing it, so did I, because I wanted to be cool, too. Here's the thing—there's nothing in life you should do just because everyone else is doing it, especially if it goes against your beliefs or values, or could potentially harm you in any way. We all have an inner voice that tells us "this is wrong." Some people listen and others don't. Take it from me. By now you know I was an expert when it came to finding ways to spin stories and situations so my life didn't seem so . . . well, let's just say pathetic.

There's an old joke that goes something like this: What are the three biggest lies in the world?

- The check is in the mail.
- I will still respect you in the morning.
- Trust me.

Over the years there have been many whale tales, but the biggest one I've ever told has been, "I'm fine." And to me, this two-word declaration outperforms the three listed above. I used that phrase to cover my real emotions from a very early age. Any child who survives an alcoholic household wears it like armor. They learn to do, say, and be whatever it takes to get through life—lies or no lies.

To do great work as an actor, it has to be based on truth. I didn't hear the truth a lot as a kid, so I learned that not telling the truth was an acceptable way to move through life. It isn't my proudest accomplishment, but it's fair to say that I lied all through the pursuit of my career and in many ways, my personal life, too. When I was starting out in the business, there were plenty of people who told me I sucked, so whenever I was told that I was great, I actually believed it. I never thought about whether or not they were being real, truthful, or authentic. I'd grown up in a home where positive reinforcement was the devil—I was so starved for approval, acceptance, and appreciation for what I brought to the table that I readily accepted any kind words, supportive statements, or adulation, even if it was a crock. Worse, I lied to myself—a lot. And I didn't realize that I might be hurting myself or others by my actions.

Though I didn't know it at the time, my first marriage was clearly based on lies—especially the ones I was telling myself. I lied by saying that it was working, that we had a great marriage, that we were happy and having fun. I had no idea what a great marriage was. My parents' marriage failed. I didn't want to get a divorce. I wanted happily ever after, so I created a story, telling myself that everything was good—that "I'm fine." I was having a relationship of my own creation versus a relationship with the person I was actually married to.

I lied about my career all of the time, too. I pretended that my career was really taking off when it was really a car stuck on the 405 Freeway because of an overturned banana truck. I told everyone I met that I was a great actress and a talented, funny comedienne when I had no idea what either of those two things really meant. Whenever someone was attentive or had the desire to show me how to be better, I had no interest. Their attempt to help me grow meant nothing to me because in my mind, I was already talented and well on my way to becoming a star.

And whenever the topic of my career did come up, I was the first to announce that I was working on something "fabulous," when I wasn't doing anything constructive. Kathleen had clients working as producers and lead actors on television series and in movies. They made time in their schedules to do the work and on screen I saw the results. Not me. I was so "busy" that I couldn't, make that *wouldn't*, make the time. What a joke, because I wasn't busy working. I was wasting time running around doing my best to appear superbusy. I ran around telling everyone how great things were going. I had meeting after meeting, filling my days running from here to there with very little to show for my efforts. In fact, I took meetings with anyone and everyone remotely associated with acting just to appear busy and important. I had a lot of "lunches" to talk about "projects" as if I had a lot of things going on, but I never really developed any of those projects. I even took my clothes to a dry cleaner where I thought I might have a chance run-in with celebrities and called that "networking."

That frenetic behavior was a choice I made because I was looking for guarantees. Life doesn't come with guarantees and neither does work. It doesn't matter how many lunches, dinners, and meetings you go to. If you're not working at the work, you're not working. Period. End of story.

4. Focus on the end result and ignore "the process."

You have to be willing to work harder than you ever thought you had to. This is what is called "the process." When you don't think you have five more minutes in your day, find it. When you think you can't do ten more sit-ups, do them. When you think you can't find the time to focus on your family, figure it out. Emerson once said, "The difference between a hero and a regular man is that a hero was braver five minutes longer."

Amen.

Be willing to be brave.

I used to have an acting teacher named Lesly Kahn who said, "Dare to suck." What she meant was, be willing to take a chance without focusing on the outcome. It took me a long time to learn to take that first step without looking for a "guarantee" to hang onto. Recording *Old School Kids Beats* was my greatest lesson in experiencing "the process." I worked extremely hard from the moment I set foot in the studio. I was willing to fail, but I wasn't willing to quit. What I discovered was that every obstacle and every challenge I faced, I could meet, fix, and rerecord if I had to. And as I progressed and persevered, the right people came into the process, too. I'd gone through a lot of flaky "beat" artists, producers, and others who talked a big game but never showed up, and it became clear they didn't care about my project.

For the first time in my life, I was on the other side of that equation.

Wait a minute. Did *I* just say that?

You might want to reverse engineer to get to step one in the process—breaking something down to understand the components in order to improve and rebuild.

If you want to get in shape, lose weight, build muscle, and strengthen your body, you have to work at it. You can't will it. You can't think yourself into shape. You have to hit the gym, eat right, and work the program hard to achieve those results. If you are always making up excuses, creating reasons why you can't, you won't.

Ever.

Never.

Instead of saying you "can't" spend those extra five minutes a day doing something that pushes you toward your goal. Watch a scene in a movie that inspires and informs you, listen to a song that moves or motivates you, read the Bible, do something positive to create a path you want to walk on. Before you know it, five minutes turns into ten and ten into fifteen. Pretty soon you will be giving 110 percent of your effort toward doing things that will help you reach your goals. Being aware of this has brought me unexpected benefits: I am more joyous and excited about things. I missed out on so many opportunities in the past because I wasn't looking at what I could learn from or give to the experience. I was only focused on what I couldn't get and what someone wouldn't give me. I didn't understand how to look for the gain in loss.

Jeff always makes fun of me for using the phrase, "It's not about the destination, it's about the journey." He thinks it's a hokey way of approaching life. *I* think it's the *only* way to get through whatever life brings our way. If you can embrace that every situation—good, bad, funny, or sad—is an opportunity for growth, you'll discover there's nothing you can't get through.

5. Present yourself in an inauthentic way and expect real results.

For the longest time, whenever I went to an audition unprepared, I couldn't understand why I wasn't getting cast in any of the roles. You might say I showed up, but I was never *really* present. I had a different goal in mind. I was extremely good at worrying about and *wanting* the job instead of walking in, looking appropriate, and *doing* the job. How you present yourself often dictates how people see you. Early in my acting career, I went on an audition for the kids' television show *Beakman's World*. I'd done so many characters over the years that I figured I could go in and wing it, be a freak and land the job. This was at a time when I was actually pretty disengaged in the process of auditioning. I did no research in advance to understand the show I was auditioning for or who would be doing the casting, and was so full of myself that I didn't much care. I knew I wanted to stand out from all of the other actors so I bought a chicken limbo apparatus that cawed, "Chicken Boooooo" every time you made it under the stick. When I went to the audition, I set up the limbo stick and began running around the room like a crazy person while doing the limbo. I honestly think the casting director considered calling the police to come escort me away to the not-so-funny farm. Thankfully, they didn't call the cops but they did ask someone to walk me out the door. At the time, I really thought the audition went well and that I had given them the best of me. Later that day, my manager called with their feedback. They told him they were worried that something was seriously wrong with me.

Showing up means different things to people, and it certainly has taken on a whole new meaning to me over the years. I spent four years on *Flipping Out* showing up, but not fully engaged. I thought it was enough to be "I'm-fun-and-I'm-here Jenni." I never once cracked open a design magazine in our early years working together. That sent a message—loud and clear—that I wasn't interested and I didn't care. I really believed that my physical presence was enough.

Believe me—it doesn't work that way.

Showing up in an *authentic* way means you are fully present, engaged, and if you've done the work, you're exhausted by the end of the day. You can't just phone it in and expect them to be impressed with your results. People began to get extremely frustrated with me because the only thing they saw me doing to move my career forward were lunches and dinners. I booked up my days, appearing to be someone who was headed down the path of success when I wasn't. I was constantly dealing with people who were successful and earning a living in show business. I was pretending to be like them minus doing the work. It was preposterous and a one-way ticket to the fast lane of failure.

6. Really thinking it's all about you.

Okay, by now you've got the idea that for a long stretch, I walked through life believing the world revolved around me, that it owed me something, and I could do no wrong. When you are cast in a role or join a company, you become part of a team. I don't think a lot of people really get the concept of teamwork. If they did, 50 percent (or more) of marriages wouldn't end up in divorce! For generations, there has been an ebb and flow of living in the "me" or the "we." When you live in the me, it's every man or woman for him or herself. When you live in the we, you can move mountains for the collective greater good. It took lots of expensive therapy for me to embrace that *it's not about me.* I know . . . this revelation came as a total shock to me, too!

Throughout my early years of auditioning, it never once occurred to me that the job I was going for was the same job that the people sitting behind the desk relied on, too. I never considered that they had a stake in the outcome—that my needs weren't their needs. I never looked at the process of auditioning as a business that required teamwork. For me, it was all about "show": "I'll show them." I was wasting their time and my connections living in the "I" and not understanding "we."

Learning to be patient is a great equalizer when it comes to understanding that there is always more than your job on the line. I had to learn to be a valuable team player and embrace the concept of protecting your boss . . . for example, covering for him so he doesn't look more germophobic than actually he is. In 2009, Jeff and I were invited to ring the opening morning bell on the New York Stock Exchange. We got this honor because someone had cancelled at the last minute.

Jeff shook a lot of hands that morning and was increasingly worried about germs. The gentleman who was escorting us through the exchange talked about the history and all of the different people who had shared this great honor. To prepare us, he said the bell rings at precisely 9:30 a.m. At 9:29:45, we needed to be on the podium, in place and ready to hit the big red button that sounds the ringing of the bell.

Jeff was all set to press the button, but as the seconds ticked down, it became a Cindy Brady moment (the episode where she freezes as the red light on the television camera is switched on). Believe it or not, Jeff froze. You can't be late when you're ringing the opening bell of the largest stock exchange in the world. I pushed the button. He immediately placed his hand over mine so we did it together. We saved the world from potential financial chaos that morning and realized that sometimes two is better than one.

7. Don't listen to your mother when she is giving you good advice.

Like most kids, it took me a long time to discover that a lot of the advice I'd rejected from my mother over the years was actually *good*. Of course, I didn't listen to her at the time, which I see now was a mistake. When I first told my mom that I wanted to marry Chris, she talked to me about the importance of marrying someone who has similar beliefs. At the time, I thought she was crazy because I really thought Chris and I had so much in common. Comedy does not a marriage make. I fought her tooth and nail, thinking she was trying to own me. Naturally, I didn't believe my mom truly understood who I was—after all, my life was supposed to be so "different" from hers.

Turns out, not this time around.

Mom instilled a strong work ethic in me from a very early age. "Work hard, because hard work pays off," she'd say.

Yeah, I didn't really listen to her on that one either.

"Jennifer, you have to present yourself in a positive way. Put yourself together when you're going out on interviews and try to sell yourself. Be happy you are unique!" she'd say.

Nope. Didn't really hear her on that solid advice.

I wanted to be the rebel who had to be her own person. Since I didn't really have the typical look I thought it would take to get noticed, I wore my hats backward and dressed in crazy costumes. Oh, I got noticed, all right—but not in the way I hoped.

There's an old saying, "Mother knows best." You may not realize it when you're young and you may not even want to accept it as you mature, but the reality is, your mom has been through life experiences and has navigated situations and circumstances you likely think she hasn't, and therefore won't give much credence to the words and advice she offers to you along the way. You may think she's being critical, judgmental, out of touch, old-fashioned, snarky, and doubting. And you may even be right. But, you have to remember she loves you and cares about the choices you're making along the way. Her approach, her tone, her manner in which she comes at a particular situation may not always jive with how you see things but this doesn't necessarily make her wrong. And it certainly doesn't always make her right. But the reality is, she likely has more insight than you're giving her credit for, so don't dismiss her words without some thought. So for all of those times I doubted you, and all the times I fought back, I now realize that being my mother was a very, very difficult job—Alice (Mom), what you did with this "juvenile delinquent" deserves an award.

In Greek, *efharisto.* (In English, thank you!)

8. Giving up the fight when you believe in something.

When *Flipping Out* was initially picked up, I felt I deserved to have some type of credit for the show. After all, *The Wannabes* gave birth to *Flipping Out.* I stood firm that I wouldn't do the show unless I got some type of co-producer credit. Even though I felt the need to stand my ground, Jeff wasn't sure I would win this battle. I couldn't let them promise me something and then take it away after I signed my agreement. If I allowed that to happen, it would have set a precedence to let the network disrespect me and my contributions. I was setting up a business relationship that I hoped would be strong, but it had to be mutually agreeable to succeed.

The executives at Bravo were clear in telling me I shouldn't expect a co-producer's credit. At the time, no one in a supporting role had that kind of credit.

"No," I said.

I believed I had a strong hand in creating the show that became Jeff's. I wanted Jeff to support me with the network. Jeff didn't give me any false hopes, but he assured me he would talk to Andy Cohen, the Executive Vice President of Original Programming and Development for Bravo. I was at a wedding in Costa Rica when Jeff e-mailed me to say he was having lunch with Andy to discuss the matter, though he reiterated that he really didn't think the network would give in. Most of the people offering me advice agreed with him. I was beyond scared, but something deep inside me knew if I didn't make the choice to step up and believe in myself how could anyone else expect to?

The next morning, I received a call saying I'd gotten what I wanted.

In Andy's book, *Most Talkative,* he writes about the lunch he and Jeff had on this very subject, saying that Jeff convinced Andy it was the right thing to do. Jeff had my back and showed me and the network that he wanted me to be a part of the show. It was a scary thing to go through, but in the end I didn't give up the fight for something I believed in. That's how I became a producer.

9. Avoid responsibility.

I always thought it would be easier to make it in Hollywood if I were blonde with big boobs and a tiny waist. I am a

Greek-American girl with curly dark hair, who used to be chubby. These were not characteristics of a Hollywood starlet. Unfortunately, I never owned my uniqueness. Instead, I used it as the reason why I wasn't getting jobs. People often said they didn't know how to categorize my look because I didn't fit any particular stereotype. I wasn't the typical "best friend" and they didn't think I was lead material either. I didn't understand the reason that no one was seeing me as a lead was because of the massive amount of responsibility that position required. I wasn't capable of being much more than a bit player due to the fact I hadn't been willing to do the work. I avoided taking any responsibility for my part in not getting the roles I desired by not showing up prepared, ready, willing, or able to deliver consistently.

One surefire way to fail is to not know about the product you are selling—especially if that product is you.

In acting, the reality is you *give* a performance. In any profession, you have the responsibility to give, give, give, and just when you think you've got nothing left to give, you have to give some more.

10. Don't write the check.

I once had a girlfriend who would spend hundreds of dollars on a T-shirt, thousands on jackets and shoes, and had a wardrobe to kill for. When I was holding her coat, watching from the sidelines of the red carpet, I dreamed of having those nice things, but I didn't feel I could, because . . . I was broke.

It took some very good advice that led me to the wonderful world of resale shopping. One of the great things about living in Los Angeles is that the consignment shops are filled with fabulous designer clothing priced at a fraction of their original cost. Welcome to high-end label heaven! For the most part, these items have only been worn a few times—if at all. At these shops, I found clothing that was once very expensive but now easy for me to afford. I bought a Burberry coat that I saw in *W Magazine* for seventy-eight dollars! At the time, that felt like a fortune, but then I remembered hearing the advice that you need to "write the check." To make money, you need to spend money and your clothes speak volumes. Pay attention to what they are saying.

I realize money is an uncomfortable topic for most people, myself included. It took me a long time to come around to understanding the value in investing in myself. Write the check for the things that you want to do and become and be willing to spend money on the people and things that will help get you there.

You might think you're already doing that, but for the real proof of where and how you are spending your money, look at your checkbook. Your checkbook is a very interesting "tell all" about your life. If you were to look at the register what would it reveal?

There's a saying, "Open their checkbook and you will see who someone is." What are you spending your money on?

I said I wanted to be a better actress but I wasn't using my resources to achieve that. I never invested in books or DVDs that might have helped me study my craft and propel my career forward. The only thing I focused on was being dissatisfied.

Looking back, I didn't spend my money on the things I said I wanted. Instead, I went out to dinner with friends where I could complain about not working. Making the decision to pursue the things I said I wanted made a huge difference. I started making money in my career and it was because I was willing to write the check.

10

Man Up: A Little Deb in All of Us

> Lots of people want to ride with you in the limo, but what you want is someone who will take the bus with you when the limo breaks down.
>
> —OPRAH WINFREY

I have a long history of creating characters that I've used over the years to help me find and then express my voice. I once pretended to be a part-time talent manager dressed as my character Gordy, who claimed his sole purpose in life was to get work for his client, the fabulously talented Jenni Pulos.

I suppose this was my homage to Andy Kaufman, who was such a genius at this type of role-play.

A very popular character I developed over the years is Deb Krux—a woman I refer to as my cousin and who was born during my early rap career. (By the way, Deb loves quoting Oprah—*see above*.) Several years ago, the *LA Times* produced

DEBBIE "DEB" CRUX
CRAFT SERVICES

Fruits, nuts, and flakes . . . guess my location!

short vignettes that aired in movie theaters around Los Angeles before the feature film. They were usually movie-industry specific, focusing on different jobs that go into making movie magic, from stuntmen to sound effects. I thought it would be funny to use Deb as a character who works the craft service (snack) table on a set. I created a short vignette that everyone loved from the start.

Deb is strong, formidable, and totally unafraid to say what she thinks! She also knows how to get things done—and fast. She isn't afraid to stand up for herself or to others. She has no filter, which is why I think Jeff Lewis (and so many of our viewers) like her so much.

Kindred spirits?

Perhaps.

Many people relate to this character; I guess that's why I am often asked to speak as Deb wherever I go.

In the beginning, Deb was just a character I only played on occasion. These days, she exists as a separate persona with Twitter and Facebook accounts. I'm not saying I have multiple personalities—there may be some people in my life who would dispute this—but Deb has been brought to life in such a way that people really do believe she exists beyond my imagination.

Deb is everything I am not. She speaks in a voice that is a good octave lower than my sometimes squeaky pitch, which must be the reason people take her more seriously. There is no mountain too high to climb with a smile, but if a smile doesn't get her there, her fierce determination and name-calling certainly will!

In fact, most people like Deb more than they do me. I know Jeff does. He is deeply amused by her. Whenever Deb is around, we tend to play around at work, finding ways to connect through her. I will admit that I fall back on humor to sometimes bait and switch Jeff, especially when I can feel the air thicken around the office. I can stay in character all day long if I have to, as long as it means getting things done and having a few laughs along the way.

Deb isn't afraid to ask for what she wants and frankly, she has taught me a thing or two about how to go about getting it. While I don't think I've used Deb's strength enough in my personal life, when it comes to work, she is there with a snap of my finger. We have a cabinetmaker we work with on *Flipping Out,* who frequently refers his brother to work on our jobs. Even though we had worked with them for thirteen years, we had never met the brother before and therefore, he didn't know any of us. They had given us a price to do some cabinetry on a project that was more than we could spend for one of our clients.

Whenever a little ball busting needs to happen around the office, we usually call in Deb to get it done. Unaware that Deb doesn't really exist, I gave the brother a call from Jeff's office and said, "Hi, this is Deb from Jeff Lewis's office. I need you to get a better price from your brother on the cabinets. He's really dicking us around. We bring you a lot of business. Make this happen!"

"Yeah, of course. Yeah, sure," he nervously responded. He had no idea he was talking to me.

"Maybe we can grab a beer sometime," I said.

"Oh, yeah. I would like that. But what I'd really like is to take that Jenni out for a beer." He was serious, too. Deb had no choice but to shut that down, and fast.

"Well, that's not going to happen, she's taken, so back off!" She was gruff and clear.

"Oh, I'm sorry. I didn't know," he said as he apologized over and over.

I felt kind of bad so I forced Deb to say, "There is another nice girl in the office that you might consider."

Later that night, he actually drunk-dialed Jeff, trying to

order a Domino's pizza at 2:00 a.m. I don't know if he was really looking for pizza or trying to make a booty call to me. Jeff wasn't happy to be awakened, but Deb took care of that little problem the next morning, calling the contractor to give him a piece of her mind. I think he felt bad, but at least we got a better price on the cabinets.

Deb handles all of the things no one else wants to confront in the office, and always gets the job done. For months, Jeff couldn't get his green recycling garbage can emptied on a regular basis. Sometimes they'd come and take the trash and other weeks they wouldn't. So finally, Deb called the waste company and said, "This is Deb from Jeff Lewis's office. Look, my boss can be a real prick. You've got to pick up the recycling trash every week. He's going to make me fill individual ziplock bags with his waste if someone doesn't get their ass over here and empty it. We have asked three times for this bullshit to be picked up. It's not getting done. Who do I have to f*** to get this green yard can emptied? I am not going to lose my job over this. It is not okay. Do you know the kind of guy I work for? Do you understand the shit I have to endure? I'll get fired for you not doing your job!"

An hour later, the waste management company showed up and the garbage was gone. They never missed another week again.

Jeff *loves* Deb. For his birthday a few years ago, he said the only thing he wanted was for Deb to work the entire day—not Jenni. So I came in dressed as Deb, and stayed in character the entire day. No one knew I was going to do this, not even the camera guys. When I got to Jeff's house, someone on the crew stopped me because they didn't recognize me in character. They went inside to ask Jeff if he was expecting a strange-looking woman. They thought I was trying to break into his house! Naturally, Jeff knew it was me, but we tried to keep it from everyone else as long as we could. I never broke character the entire day. None of the footage from that ever made it to air. But if it had, you would have seen a very different dynamic between Jeff and Deb than you do between Jeff and Jenni. Very often, Jeff and Deb drove around in Jeff's car in complete silence. That doesn't happen very often when I'm in the car. And when Jeff and Deb did talk, it was mostly about how annoying Jenni is—always talking about her big auditions, jobs she didn't get, and how delusional I . . . I mean *she*, is.

Jeff and Deb got along great because Deb doesn't talk about herself, her personal issues, her upcoming plans, auditions that aren't happening, or dating. She just comes to work and gets things done. Deb isn't afraid to speak her mind, and neither is Jeff, so when they get together, I think there's a mutual respect that he and I don't share on the same level. They're a lot more alike than we are.

WWDS (WHAT WOULD DEB SAY?)

Just get it done.

Whatever doesn't kill me, had better start running.

Kick yourself in the ass, or someone else will.

Man up, you pussy.

The difference between *try* and *triumph* is a little
  "umph."
Buzz off.
Keep your problems to yourself. Twenty percent don't
  care, eighty percent are glad you have 'em.
Learn a lesson from your dog. No matter what life brings
  you, kick some grass over that shit and move on.
We are all born dumb, but you have to work real hard to
  stay stupid.
I have not met Mr. Right yet . . . but I have met Mr.
  Rude, Mr. Cheap, and Mr. Married.
If assholes could fly, this place would be an airport.
. . . and she means it.

Deb says things with complete confidence and isn't apol-
ogetic for her behavior. At one point, Jeff turned to me dressed
as Deb and said, "Nobody is ever going to want to sleep with
you again!"

Deb isn't a big talker—she is more of a doer. She doesn't
say much, and mostly only speaks when she needs to. But
what she says matters and has the intended impact. Of course,
because of her rough-around-the-edges masculinity, most
people think Deb is a lesbian—but she's not. At least I don't
think so; she's never told me she is. She's just a tough woman
who doesn't take crap from anyone.

She gets pissed off all the time because she doesn't have
health insurance. She only works part-time, so she isn't eligi-
ble, but Jeff doesn't offer health insurance to anyone except

Zoila anyway. And Deb could really use it because she blew her knee out in a softball accident. Plus, she smokes, which isn't helping her lungs much either. Deb is the only person Jeff lets smoke in his office. He is enamored with her and lets her get away with everything!

Deb speaks the words I am often afraid to say. As you now know, I am a people pleaser who avoids saying things that make a situation really uncomfortable, but ultimately, sometimes those are the things we all need to hear. Like it or not, there is a need for confrontation in life. Through Deb, I've discovered that confrontation often leads to progress. I've never been that person, but Deb sure is. She is straightforward and unafraid to speak the truth or her mind about things as she sees them. Who hasn't secretly wished to be more assertive, less afraid, and willing to take more chances? Perhaps some may see that kind of behavior as being a bitch. I see it as no-nonsense and a much simpler way of life.

Deb works hard for what she has. She doesn't worry about a thing—ever. I could use a little of her BS-free way of thinking.

I thought it might be fun to get Deb's take on life and living inside this crazy bitch's body. So I sat down and interviewed her for the book. *Note to lawyers: Although Jenni has signed a nondisclosure with Jeff on what she can and cannot write about in this book, Deb has signed no such agreement and therefore is exercising her right to Freedom of Speech, under the First Amendment to the United States Constitution.

ME: Thanks for sitting with me, Deb. Let's get started. What is your take on me?

DEB: You've got a pretty good heart and appear to be extremely determined. I like that you've become more fearless, but holy hell, you can be whiny and complaining. I am so tired of hearing you talk about all of the parts you didn't get and the bullshit reasons why! I mean, just do it. This poor-me crap is old already. When you want something, you've got to stop your complaining and just do it. When you're done, you can go and have a cigarette or whatever it is you do to celebrate.

ME: Don't hold back, tell me how you really feel!

DEB: Okay. You want the truth? Here it is. You can be a little bitch sometimes. Do you think that squeaky voice is going to get you what you want? There are enough fruits and nuts in L.A. running around taking bullshit meetings that never amount to anything. I am busy, too, and you know what? I work for a prick that doesn't offer health insurance, but you don't hear me whining about it.

ME: Speaking of bosses, what's your take on Jeff Lewis?

DEB: Jeff and I see eye to eye. He likes things the way he likes it. That's his thing, so just deal with it. I don't say a lot. I keep my head down and just do my work. When there is an altercation, it falls on me to break it up. A lot of people in that office have their heads up their ass. I can't deal with other people's incompetence any more than he can, but he is a little bit of a bitch, too. He is too crazy with his OCD crap, lining up his garbage cans and all of the bottles facing out in his fridge perfectly straight. I guess there is an ass for every saddle.

ME: What do you think are my strengths?

DEB: Your tits.

ME: Thank you!

DEB: You are good with people. I'm not really like that. There's another thing Jeff and I have in common. I am better with animals—like a nice Rottweiler or German shepherd. I had a guinea pig growing up that I trained to attack people who pissed me off. My dad named her "Lady."

ME: What are my weaknesses?

DEB: You worry and complain about stuff that doesn't ever end up happening or existing. Not doing the work but talking and complaining about it, making people the enemy when they aren't, causing more crap for yourself than you need. If you don't like something about your situation, take action and change it. Don't cry about it like a baby.

ME: What's it like to see me happy?

DEB: It's nice. All of that divorce wah, wah, wah stuff was getting old. A lot of people get divorced. It makes you like 52 percent of the women in this country. Deal with it. I understand that you suffered pain and humiliation. Everyone has pain, but you eventually pulled yourself up. It's time you found happiness because you needed to calm the frick down. I like dealing with you a lot more these days than I did when you were a selfish train wreck. It's like you've cut through the weeds and put in a nice landing strip. Plus, you found a great guy who has a nice ass.

ME: How do you get through tough times?

DEB: I go for a drive in my muscle car or watch Animal Planet or the Game Show Network. Life is short. You need to live it and appreciate every day.

ME: One last question, Deb . . . What message would you want to give the reader as your takeaway?

DEB: Man up. Get your shit together and don't complain. Take responsibility for yourself. If you're going to be a pussy, own it. No excuses.

11

Failing Forward and Lessons Learned

> I've failed over and over and over again in my life and that is why I succeed.
>
> —MICHAEL JORDAN

I have a strong appreciation for the benefits of taking a wrong turn along the way.

When I was a junior in high school, I ran for student body treasurer and was elected by a landslide. This easy victory had me convinced that I could be student body president in my senior year, no problem. I was a pretty popular kid and my opponent was well liked, too. I gave my speech, which may have been a little too animated compared to her straightforward, no-nonsense, non-gimmicky approach. Looking back, gimmicks have never really served me, but I kept right on using them because I thought they made me memorable, lovable, and would land me the job. I thought I had the election in the bag, but I didn't. I lost by five votes to her. Someone told me they saw one of my best friends cast a vote against me. How could she have done that? I was crushed and embarrassed. The defeat paralyzed me with fear. I couldn't believe I'd lost the election. As a way to redeem myself, I ran for senior class president against a kid no one really knew. He was a quiet loner. I upped my gimmicks in my senior class speech believing there was no way I wouldn't beat this guy. I had a chart with stick figures and points of why it was so obvious that I should win. I was shocked when the results were announced over the loudspeaker at school: I'd lost. I thought there had to be a mistake. I wanted a recount. Something had to be wrong.

Out of desperation, I decided to run for class senator. There was no official election for this role. It was more of an appointment. For sure I wouldn't lose. Most great achievements come from meandering paths of misjudgment and false turns. I've heard author John C. Maxwell call it *failing forward*. This election experience was the beginning of a chronic series of failing-forward events that would end up shaping my future.

When we fail, we have the option of allowing that failure to hold us back or propel us forward. When you fail backward, you usually play the victim, blaming others for your mistakes. When you fail forward, you learn to take responsibility, learning from each mistake and understanding that each failure is a part of the process that leads to progress. In the end, failure leaves you with two choices: quit or learn and move forward. If you quit, you fail backward. If you choose to persevere with the knowledge you've gained, you fail forward.

The point is, you will have many failures and setbacks in order to achieve your goals . . . guaranteed! It's how you choose to deal with failure that will determine your time in the winner's circle. Look at life's setbacks and learn from your mistakes. Learn to embrace failure when it happens and think of it as the breakfast of champions! Champions are not spared failure. They are made by their response to it.

When the real estate market crashed in 2008, a lot of developers were stuck holding too many properties that suddenly became more overhead than they could carry. There was a flood of inventory on the market and very few qualified buyers. When you're in the business of flipping homes, you can't hold on to a property for too long because you rely on the income from the sale to fund the next venture. Some developers went into panic mode because most were heavily leveraged, which forced them to unload their real estate holdings at bargain basement prices in order to pay down some of their big debt. Other developers in L.A. weren't as brave as Jeff. They thought they could ride out the dismal real estate market. And a lot of them lost everything.

When Jeff realized the market was crashing, he could have panicked, but he didn't. He put aside his ego, lowered his prices, and got out fast, without taking as hard a financial hit as many others in the business. Even though he felt the financial pinch, he did the right thing based on the state of the market. At the time, I think Jeff was terrified that he'd failed because he had to sell the houses for less money than he could have if it had been an up market. But I didn't see his actions as a failure at all. I saw his reaction to the market as courageous and savvy. There is no such thing as a life or career that doesn't have ups and downs. Ask any working actor in Hollywood, and they'll tell you that like most businesses, you have to ride the waves. Real estate is no exception.

The most successful people on the planet know when to fold their cards and cut their losses. However, the 2008 real estate crash was the first time I ever saw Jeff outwardly appear vulnerable. He loved flipping houses and he felt like that had been stripped away from him. Jeff was making a great living and then one day, the market changed and everything stopped.

Well, not *everything*.

Like most unexpected changes, when one door closes you have to believe a window usually opens.

Jeff's liquidation allowed him the opportunity to move into another area of interest he'd been eyeing but hadn't gotten around to—design. By making this shift, he successfully redefined his passion and was able to express his talent in a new way. I don't know if Jeff would have walked this path had the market not forced his decision to do so. In the end, it worked in his favor because he now has a thriving design business that brings him a tremendous amount of satisfaction as well as another outlet for his immense creativity.

Don't let failure stop you from pursuing or living your dreams. The key to overcoming failure is not to wallow in it for more time than you need—for me, that's somewhere around thirty minutes—because you are wasting precious time. You paid for that failure, so you may as well take that knowledge and do something much greater with it than feeling sorry for yourself.

> Success consists of going from failure to failure without loss of enthusiasm.
>
> —WINSTON CHURCHILL

Owning the failure so you can own the forward—that is what failing forward is all about. I failed forward in some very strange ways, especially when I was hired to sell sausages around 1997 at the farmer's market in L.A. I learned that I would sell more if I stroked the sausages. It wasn't really my idea. Customers asked me to do it. As an aspiring actress, I thought of it as performance art. Okay, maybe that was a bit of a push, but hey, it worked. I sold more sausages than anyone else.

The first real job I landed that made me feel as if I had finally "made it" was a show I co-hosted with Dr. Drew Pinsky for the Discovery Health Channel. It was like the show *Love Line*, and I was the female Adam Corolla. It was a very exciting gig because this was the first time a studio sent a car for me and I would have my own dressing room.

I had arrived.

I was in show business.

It was like a dream come true.

My first assignment was a masturbation party in Florida.

I actually had to interview couples while they were masturbating.

Since this was a Discovery Health show, the participants were clothed, but they had ticklers and other toys they were using to help them climax. One older man told me that when he was close to climax, he would say, "Wheezy Peezy."

Other shows I got to take part in included watching a man get his balls pierced and a woman who had a necklace that said, "I ♥ (fill in blank)" rhymes with "Rum." This was not the Hollywood break I thought it was. Most everything I ever planned in my life never seemed to work out the way I thought it would. There's an old saying: "We make plans and God laughs." Well, God sure does have a good sense of humor because I am certain my life has offered more than a fair share of laughs up there in heaven. Yes, I believe in heaven.

The shows never aired. The series was reconfigured into a new concept, reshot and renamed, *Strictly Sex with Dr. Drew*. It was a very clinical show that didn't call for a funny sidekick. That was probably a good thing.

I could have been deterred by that experience, but I wasn't. I became more determined than ever to prove I could make it. When something looks like it's going in one direction, it can actually be moving in the other and before you know it, become something else altogether. The important thing to remember is to never give up. Despite the letdowns, I tried to make the best of every situation I was in, trusting it would lead me in the direction of getting what I wanted.

The only time I couldn't get into character for a job was when I tried my hand . . . my voice . . . at being a phone sex operator. When I applied for the . . . position . . . job . . . the manager told me I would be very good at it because I sounded like I was extremely young. Right then I knew I was out of my comfort zone. Still, I thought it might be fun or at the very least, interesting. As hard as I tried, though, I couldn't go through with it. It was pretty much the moment the woman next to me was talking to her caller about unspeakable things while ordering her meat lover's pizza in the background that I knew this was not for me.

And then there was a time that an ex-manager (under-score ex, you'll see why in a minute) had booked me to do a video for a product called, "The Dick Towel." One side of the towel had a rather large erect penis, and the other side showed the same penis after getting out of the water. Think "shrink-age." My manager actually took pictures of me with the towel and put them on the Internet without letting me know. I didn't need dick towel photos out there. Even I didn't want that kind of attention!

I accidently left the dick towel at my mom's house during a Christmas visit. I was horrified when she randomly appeared in her kitchen wearing the dick towel, shrinkage side out. She had no idea what image was on the towel she was wrapped in and I've never been able to get the image of her in the dick towel out of my mind.

Frustrated by the "shrinkage" on the acting side of life, I continued my budding rap career in 2005 by joining a group when one of my theater friends from UCLA had to drop out. This group eventually morphed into another act called Hot N the Biscuit. Although we originally started out as a JAP Rap group, singing songs about Jewish-American Princess issues, such as "Yoga Ho," our style of rap changed over time. We went

Backstage at the Knitting Factory before a Hot N the Biscuit show—2003.

from class to crass, with a repertoire of new songs about funky undies, Bob Saget, and Punani. We began to get a little attention for our music, performing at the Telluride Film Festival, the Viper Room, the Knitting Factory, Luna Park, and the Laugh Factory. We shot music videos, released a CD, had an album on iTunes, and enjoyed the run while it lasted. I loved performing and doing our shows, but I wasn't growing or going in the direction I wanted to go in. It's hard to be taken seriously as an actress, especially when I was spending my time breaking it down in the street, wearing dreads and backward baseball hats.

For many years, I didn't think working as an actress was something I had to give to myself—I believed it was something other people would give me. I felt my career was totally in their hands. That is a lot of power to hand over to people who are, frankly, concerned with their own careers so they can pay *their* bills to support *their* families.

I believed a career was like a fancy vending machine where I could simply push a button and get a treat. I had no idea that if you really want something, you have to fully commit to it, show up, be present, do the work and stop complaining! I didn't understand that like anything we do, you have to keep building momentum to see results. Eventually, someone will take notice and progress will be made. I spent years watching friends of mine get work, I saw their careers growing, but I couldn't understand why the same wasn't happening for me. Did I bother to really look at what they were doing to acheive their results? No. Of course not! I learned I had to persevere with the work I initially *didn't want to do.* Earlier in my career, if I did the work and didn't get an immediate result, I gave up.

Finally, I decided to get serious and focus on what I wanted. I spent two and a half months working like a serious professional, doing the work and being prepared. I did research, showed up early instead of being perpetually late, prepared for my scenes, and made sure I was totally ready to do the work. I began to care about the people I was meeting and showed my appreciation for them by honoring who they were and supporting that the work I was seeking was their project, not mine. Learning to be sensitive to the people I work with and for maximized my chances of being SEEN.

During those couple of very focused months, seemingly, out of the blue, CBS called and asked me to come in and read for their head of casting. This was the first time I didn't go into an audition with the mind-set that just because I showed up and did a good job, there would *and* should be a positive outcome. The reality of the acting profession is that you have to go in, and audition over and over. Then, maybe, just maybe, someone will take notice of your work. And when they do, it has all been worth it.

In my personal life, failing forward also helped me close a chapter with Chris. Several years after we divorced, I unexpectedly ran into him at my local dry cleaner. It was divine intervention because that was the day I knew that chapter of my life was over. Looking back, I realized that I married this man who was really just my buddy and someone I loved performing with. We certainly had a lot of fun, and from the outside looking in, people probably thought we had a wonderful relationship when, in fact, we had no relationship. Chris and I had fun, but when, the going got tough, he ran.

I often look back on the characters we created together, especially Gordy and Lolly. It's so strange that these characters took on a life of their own, and when Chris and I broke up, that project disappeared, which made me almost as sad as losing my husband. Does that make me sound shallow?

Maybe, but it's the truth.

Ten years of my life came full circle at the dry cleaner that day. Oddly, Chris had become nothing more than a stranger. I felt nothing when I saw him, and ultimately, that was a good thing.

I had no regrets.

No remorse.

No sadness.

Just nothing.

And that in and of itself felt good—*really* good, because it meant I'd gotten through that moment of my life and was willing to stand in truth because I had accepted that we failed.

For me, learning to fail forward became a journey of embracing the unknown. It meant having to refocus on the positive things that were happening all around me, events I couldn't see until I learned to open my eyes and appreciate my life—as challenging as it was to me—and understand that it wasn't all that bad. In fact, I could honestly say it was . . . good.

12

Finding Guidance, Wisdom, Family, and a Home

> What can we do to promote world peace? Go home and love your family.
>
> —MOTHER THERESA

Out of total desperation, and I think as a way to help me get out of my funk and bad dating machine, my sister persuaded a friend to give my number to a guy named Jonathan, who they'd been trying to fix me up with for some time. He was doing his sports medicine fellowship at Kerlan Jobe in Los Angeles, where the friend's husband was one of the partners. I'd known their family for years. After seeing how heartbroken I was, they'd hoped I'd meet someone. When I didn't, they kept mentioning this nice Greek doctor but seemed hesitant to pass on my number. I suppose they worried that if we didn't hit it off, it would be awkward. I was sad, hurt, and scared for so long, but around this time,

I was actually near being at peace with the idea of being alone. I wasn't desperate to be in a relationship and was actually feeling, perhaps for the first time in my life, comfortable in my own skin. I guess you could say I got out of my own way and embraced whatever the future held for me.

There were a few lame attempts to set up a casual meeting with Jonathan that never seemed to pan out. Thankfully, my sister got involved and convinced our friends that we were all adults and if it didn't work out, it would be fine. But if it did, well, they would have given me the best gift I could have ever asked for. She may have bullied them a little, but they finally gave in and passed along my number.

Jonathan called a few days later and asked me out. It was your typical blind date, except this time it was awesome. Five hours later, we found ourselves closing down the restaurant. I didn't go into the evening expecting anything. I suspected he would be a nice guy, but I had no idea I would find my soul mate that night. Our first date was the best night of my life. It was effortless, calm yet exciting. It was the most peaceful and safe I had ever felt—and I've held on to those feelings ever since.

My next "official" date with Jonathan was attending a Halloween party. I dressed as a "hot dog on a stick" girl. It was by far one of my favorite Halloween costumes ever because they're very hard to come by. You have to work at Hot Dog on a Stick to get one. Jonathan showed up dressed as Richard Simmons. He didn't know a soul in the room—and didn't care what anyone thought. He was fearless and full of fun.

Our second date—
Jonathan and I on
Halloween—2009.

This guy's alright! I thought.

We got serious pretty fast after that date. Maybe it was his striped dolphin short shorts and rhinestone-studded tank top that did it for me, but I was hooked.

I wanted someone who cared about his family, was responsible, present, and kind, and someone who accepted me for who I am. Jonathan was all of that and more. He loves his work and I could relate to that. I have a great respect for what he has chosen to do. Talk about someone who had to do the work! He's been in the library studying for twenty years! Over time, I got to witness how great Jonathan is with his patients. He goes the extra mile in everything he does, which has kept him moving forward in his career, following in the footsteps of his amazing father, who was also a gifted physician.

From the moment we met, Jonathan and I complemented each other in a way I had never experienced. I am who I am in my relationship with Jonathan because of what I learned when my first marriage failed. Experience gave me the opportunity to have a new and healthy relationship. Suddenly, I wanted to put Jonathan first and if he put me first, we were definitely headed into something long lasting. I am sure if I hadn't opened myself up to the possibilities of being alone, I would never have been able to invite someone as wonderful as Jonathan into my life.

Jonathan and I dated for about a year, throughout his fellowship in L.A. Things were going great for both of us. He was fine-tuning his skills as a surgeon and my career was growing. As his fellowship came to an end, we were faced with a decision neither of us wanted to talk about. It was time for Jonathan to go back to his hometown of Chicago, where he was set to resume his medical practice.

Chicago!

I needed to be in Los Angeles for my work.

Chicago!

Jonathan needed to be in Chicago for his work.

It's a good thing I keep my therapist's number on my speed-dial. I wasn't sure how to handle this dilemma. I'd come into the relationship with a boatload of issues, especially my fear of abandonment. If I'd had it my way, I wouldn't let Jonathan leave. My therapist helped me understand that just because he was going back to Chicago, it didn't mean the relationship had to end. She encouraged me to allow him the freedom to go back to Chicago and told me that if I didn't, I'd surely lose him down the road. He'd have to come back on his terms for our relationship to work long term.

This was going to be a really hard exercise in patience, understanding, love, and trust. I wasn't sure I was up to the challenge. I was still in a place where negative comments were validated and positive ones often dismissed.

My therapist yelled at me a few times. (Yes, I paid someone to yell at me.)

My mother was greatly relieved when I found Jonathan. I don't think a parent truly rests until their child is settled in his or her own life. I think my mom is secretly proud of what I've accomplished in my career these days. She still won't give me the satisfaction of saying it to me, but I've been told by sources that she goes to the hair salon and brags about her daughter, the actress. She is thrilled that I found someone like Jonathan to love and with whom I planned to share my life.

When my mom got into a car accident in the fall of 2011, at first no one thought it was serious, but then her brain began to bleed, making it a touch-and-go situation for a few days. When Jonathan and I went to visit her in the hospital, she was very out of it when we arrived, but not so much so that she couldn't manage to hand her hoop earring to Jonathan and say, "Jonathan, take this ring and marry her now before I die." Jonathan didn't seem fazed by her request, but from where I stood, marriage wasn't in our immediate plans. It's funny that even at death's door, my mom found a way to push as only a Greek (or Jewish, Catholic, etc.) mother can. When Mom was well on her way to recovery, I jokingly said, "You probably staged this whole hospital thing!"

She had bought so many ten-dollar candles to light at church, the Narthex (front of the Greek church) was aglow. These expensive candles are for Easter, death, and weddings, and my mother was doing everything in her power to make God aware that she wanted this doctor for her daughter.

My relationship with Jonathan grew slowly. I wasn't in a hurry to get remarried and this new patience was trickling over into all areas of my life. And guess what? It was having a positive impact!

And even as dysfunctional as Jeff and I are, we have built something meaningful together with our shows and the work we do. This was exactly what I needed to do with Jonathan. I needed to take a step back and assess what I wanted to change, in order to be strong and supportive of him—to put his needs over my own. For the first time in my life, that meant walking a positive and honest road and having the courage to stay on it.

Jonathan and I spent long days and nights talking through the logistics and decided that we'd commute between Los Angeles and Chicago as often as possible. Neither of us wanted to let go of what we had. If things progressed, we'd have to make some choices. But time was on our side. We could test the water and see how a long-distance relationship felt.

It was hard but not impossible.

We spent the next year flying to see each other whenever our schedules allowed. I spent as much time in Chicago as I could, especially when I was in between shooting *Flipping Out*. When I couldn't get to Chicago, Jonathan and I would take a long weekend away, like the time we met in Scottsdale. But the most unforgettable trip we took came as a total surprise. Jonathan wouldn't tell me anything about where we were going except that I needed to pack a bag with something nice to wear for dinner and a bathing suit.

Jonathan is a romantic man, so when he told me we were going on an adventure one Sunday, I knew something exciting was in store. We hopped into the car and drove north of Los Angeles to Santa Barbara, where we attended services at a local Greek church. The church was set back on a hill in the mountains with the most spectacular view of the sea.

At the church coffee hour after the service, we met an eighty-six-year-old Greek woman and her friend. Just like my relatives, they force-fed us.

"Your husband needs to eat . . ." she said, looking at Jonathan.

"He is my boyfriend," I said, trying to politely correct her.

"Why isn't he your husband?" she asked.

Hmmm. Good question.

"We are dating, you know, taking it slow," I said, barely believing myself as the words fell from my lips.

"Life is too short. If you are in love, get married!" the woman responded before turning away.

She had a point.

Jonathan seemed slightly uncomfortable with the exchange, so I didn't turn it into a topic of conversation beyond saying how cute and sweet these two women were.

After leaving the church, I didn't know where we were going until I saw the signs pointing us toward the San Ysidro Ranch. If you don't know about this fabulous place, it is where Jacqueline and John F. Kennedy honeymooned. It's one of the most romantic spots on the planet. Jonathan had reserved a beautiful cottage with a private patio and its own Jacuzzi.

As soon as we got settled, Jonathan turned to me and said, "Get dressed and be ready by four-thirty." I thought that 4:30 seemed too early for dinner, but I wanted to go with the flow so I did exactly what I was told.

Jonathan took my hand and led me upstairs to a gate that opened to the upper lawn of this beautiful ranch nestled into the foothills of the mountain range. In one direction, there was nothing but luscious green lawn; in the other, an endless horizon of ocean. It was one of the most perfect spots I had ever set foot on.

Jonathan timed our arrival perfect to the setting sun. What he didn't count on was a man sitting by himself on the only park bench on the lawn. I could tell that Jonathan was getting nervous—which made me nervous, too.

Is he going to do it here? I thought.

Jonathan asked the man if he'd mind taking a picture of us. The man explained that he was at the ranch with his wife celebrating their thirtieth wedding anniversary. Something told me it was no accident that this man was at the remote area of the resort at the same time we were. He was a lovely image of hope and happiness for the future.

Jonathan began to recite a verse from the Bible that spoke about love. Every word was directly from his heart. He said I inspired him and made him want to be a better person. He told me he'd been waiting his whole life for this day to come—to stand before me, his best friend. Just before he knelt down, he looked at me and said, "I am going to get down on my knee now . . .

"Jennifer Michelle Pulos, will you marry me?"

"*YES! YES! YES!*" I couldn't help myself. I never really expected this would happen to me. Though I wanted to be married, I never thought the fairy tale would be my story.

He slipped the most beautiful diamond ring on my finger.

> Love bears all things, believes all things, hopes all things,
> endures all things. Love never fails.
>
> —CORINTHIANS 13:4–8

We called his parents first and shared our news. His mom was lovely, saying that everyone in his family was so happy for us. His father told Jonathan to "take care of that fine young lady for the rest of your life." Jonathan assured his dad that he would.

When we called my mom, she screamed for a solid minute! Hallelujah! After all, she finally got what she always hoped for—another doctor for a son-in-law! Next, I sent Jeff a text message with a picture of my ring and sent Andy Cohen a text breaking the news. Andy was so sweet, asking if he could mention my engagement on his show, *Watch What Happens Live*, that night. Of course I said yes. . . ."Breaking news everyone. My girl Jenni Pulos just got engaged! I love a happy ending!"

I knew that everyone at Bravo would be happy for me. No one wanted my first marriage to end the way that it did, but I was certain they'd be delighted at the way things turned out.

Jeff texted back and said, "I couldn't be more excited for you! I'm now so glad I broke up your first marriage."

"So am I, and I love you for temporarily ruining my life," I wrote.

"You're welcome for temporarily ruining your life on national television. Your mom needs to call and thank me ASAP," he responded.

"She will be calling you—she will be screaming." I knew she would be.

"All of the praying has finally paid off . . ." he texted.

"It has!" I was so happy to share this exchange.

When the initial shock wore off, Jonathan took me to dinner in a private old adobe room in the main building of the hotel that had a fireplace and lots of history. There were beautiful flowers everywhere.

It was perfect.

Jonathan kept taking out his iPhone throughout dinner and using his flashlight app to shine it on my ring.

"Watch it sparkle!" he said, beaming from ear to ear.

As the evening went on, I looked at Jonathan and realized that we can never be certain about what life will bring our way at any given moment—but now I knew—without a doubt, what real love is.

When someone unconditionally cares for you and you for them, it is overwhelming. I'm so grateful and appreciative of every moment that brought me to this realization. It's a reminder that no matter what we go through, whether it's a bad breakup, a divorce, or even an illness, we should never give up hope. Your situation may look dark from the inside—it did for me! We all go through bad times and our hearts get broken. If it hadn't been for Jeff installing the cameras in his office, my life would have never taken the unexpected twists and turns it did to bring me here—now.

Week after week, people watched my marriage unravel. But now, they would have the chance to watch the next chapter of my life begin.

I found someone that I love and with whom I wanted to share the rest of my life—and, if we were lucky and blessed, start a family. I don't know that Jonathan and I would have clicked if I'd met him right after the demise of my first marriage because I wasn't ready to welcome a man like him into my life. I had to be ready to give and accept the kind of love I feel everyone deserves.

I'd been given a lot of second chances over the years, especially in my career, and now, I was being given a second chance at love. I was finally in a place where I could embrace what was in front of me and be okay with whatever life brought my way.

I'd finally become comfortable with who I am—flaws and all. When you are a better version of yourself, you become a more positive influence for the people around you. I had a career, good health, and most of all a man who really loves me. As I sat at dinner with Jonathan the night we were engaged, my life felt . . . *perfect*.

To completely cheapen the moment, I formally announced our engagement that night, on Twitter.

"Today is a beautiful day. The man I love has asked me to be his wife!"

Later that night, Jonathan presented two more rings for my dogs, Lulu's and Janet's, collars because he wasn't just marrying me . . . he was marrying them, too. Now *there's* a man who knows the way to his woman's heart!

Two girls waiting for their rings—Janet and Lulu.

13

OPA! It's Chic to Marry a Greek

> For I know the plans I have for you," declares the Lord,
> "plans to prosper you and not to harm you, plans to
> give you hope and a future.
>
> —JEREMIAH 29:11

Jonathan and I were married on May 27, 2012. Our wedding was what many people have described to me as "a dream." I know that sounds Velveeta, but I really felt like that. Jeff used to tease me about it all the time, even joking that "someday, you'll find a nice Greek doctor . . ." sarcastically, as if it would never happen. Well, as they say, dreams really do come true! Thanks for putting it out there in the universe for me, Jeff!

To be totally fair, planning the wedding was extremely stressful. When I married the first time, not only was I just a kid, my mom and sister took the reins and planned the whole shebang. It felt as if I just kind of showed up in my gown ready to take that walk down the aisle. It could have been someone else's wedding—but it wasn't. It was mine.

As if planning my own big fat Greek wedding wasn't enough pressure, choosing to do it on *Flipping Out* simply added a little extra fuel to the already fanning flames. In a way, it was a wonderful decision to share my bliss with our faithful viewers. On the other hand, it heightened the need to get everything right. Everyone involved would be exposed, putting more stress on our families and friends.

There were several moments along the way where I wavered on wanting Bravo to film my wedding. Maybe it would be better to start off this marriage out of the public eye? You see, the fallout from that public dirty laundry debacle was horrible. Week after week, everyone saw me coming apart at the seams. But as time passed, they also got to see me put my life back together again. If anything, I wanted to share that my pain and suffering had led me to a place that I had never dared to imagine. There are plenty of people in the world who go through a terrible breakup—but if the collapse of my first marriage helped just one person out there believe they would get through their own frightening journey, then I am grateful things happened the way they did.

Jonathan and I discussed the ups and downs of allowing Bravo access to this very intimate setting. I wasn't completely secure with exposing my relationship, my beliefs, or even my parents to the public without a safety net. After talking it through, Jonathan and I both agreed that the wedding was bigger than us and if publicly sharing it with others was a means of inspiration, then it was the right thing to do. I told Jonathan that once we agreed to it, there could be no second-guessing our decision. As we gave it more and more thought, we began to feel as if I had an obligation to share the good things happening in my life every bit as much if not more than the bad stuff. So whenever those waves of doubt washed over me, I'd remind myself to be okay with my decision to share my wedding on camera.

Before I finally agreed to allow the wedding to be filmed, I went to the executives at Bravo and made them promise that Jonathan and I would be protected. I didn't want cameras looking for dysfunctional drama. To be totally honest, I was a beast about this concern because deep down, I was actually terrified that anything could happen. That was the nontrusting, scared little girl in me who still felt a little burned by the events that led to my divorce. There I was telling Jonathan to trust the decision when inside, I wasn't trusting it at all.

I wasn't being a hypocrite.

Worrying is in my DNA.

Thankfully, Jonathan understands that about me. I have often thought that one of the reasons Jonathan and I work so well together as a couple is because we understand truths about our family dysfunction, especially worrying too much. We often remind each other that "there is no *there*, there" when we spend too much time worrying about things that are out of our control. Even so, we both still struggle with it all the time.

As we created out guest list, the number kept growing and growing until it got so big, even I started questioning all of the names on it. I have always been the kind of girl who loves to invite everyone I know to my parties. I realize everyone isn't like that, but I am, which meant we were staring down the barrel of 450 invitations being sent out.

I feared the weekend wouldn't feel intimate with so many people, but I knew in my heart that everyone coming would have a great time. One thing I know for sure is that Deb should have stepped in and made sure less people were invited to the wedding! She hated the idea of having so many guests!

We decided to have the wedding in Chicago, where Jonathan and most of his family live. Jonathan would be making the ultimate sacrifice after our wedding, by giving up his burgeoning medical practice and moving to Los Angeles to be with me. He'd have to start all over again, which was the scary and daunting reality he was facing. Even though Jonathan offered to have the wedding in L.A., it didn't feel right. I wanted to throw the biggest, best good-bye wedding for his family and friends so they could celebrate our new beginning instead of being sad that Jonathan was leaving them.

We were interested in several reception venues. I wanted a room with a breathtaking view of the Chicago skyline. I imagined lots of windows overlooking the cityscape with beautiful twinkling lights as far as the eye could see. One of the last places we looked at was the Radisson Blu Hotel. Jonathan's mom had read an article in a Chicago paper about the massive renovation the hotel had just undergone. We decided to go check it out. The second we walked into the ballroom, I knew we had found our location.

"This is it . . ." I whispered to Jonathan.

The room was spectacularly modern, large enough to accommodate our crowd and was floor to ceiling windows. Even though it wasn't on a high floor, the view was awesome. There was even an outdoor balcony that wrapped all the way around the room, so our guests could take in the magnificence of the city at night. This was the day I met Chad Jackson, the director of catering for the hotel, who was also a wedding planner. Chad and I clicked right away. He seemed to understand what it was I was looking for and how to take my dream wedding and turn it into a reality. Don't forget, I didn't have anything to do with planning my first wedding and even though I was ignorant as to what it takes to pull off a wedding of this magnitude, this time I wanted to be an integral part of the process. I didn't realize what I was getting myself into, but Chad sure did. (Thank you, Chad.)

The first meeting Chad set up was with a company called HMR Designs, an amazing Chicago-based design company. I also asked Jeff to come to Chicago and give me his insights. I thought it might be nice to involve him in the planning. I wanted Jeff's support and deep down, believed he'd get excited by being a part of the process.

When we walked into the giant HMR warehouse, I thought I had stumbled into Santa's workshop for brides. There were so many people running around, making flower arrangements, moving furniture, and packing up lights. The whole room smelled like the most delicious bouquet of fresh flowers. I think there must have been something intoxicating in that scent because I felt like Dorothy must have in the poppy fields. I was standing in the Land of Oz for brides to be and feeling like I could spend, spend, spend.

Weeeeee!

I said yes to everything I saw!

The team at HMR set up a room especially designed for our wedding that was staged behind a set of double doors. I felt like a contestant on *Let's Make a Deal.* "I'll take door number one, please!" When they swung the large wooden doors open, look out! I instantly felt prettier, sexier, and freer than ever! It was magical.

I walked into the perfectly set room and was immediately greeted by a custom-designed pattern for our dance floor. Next, they showed me the water wall, then the table settings, and finally, the centerpieces.

"I want one of everything!" I squealed with happiness.

That's pretty much about the time that Jeff jumped in and said, "Hold on. Slow down."

Reality check time, courtesy of Mr. Jeff Lewis.

Chad and I walked out of the room to talk price. I nearly choked on the first figure he gave me.

"Thanks for showing me everything I can't have . . ." I said like a heartbroken child on Christmas day who didn't get any of the toys on her list. Chad could see the disappointment in my eyes. Okay, I probably poured the puppy dog look on a little strong to see if there was any wiggle room. And guess what? It worked! I reluctantly gave up the water wall and some other compromises so I could have two chocolate fountains. Oh yeah, one for milk and the other for dark. That is how this girl rolls. Jeff ribbed me for weeks about how tacky the fountains were, but I didn't care. (Thought you might like to know that on the night of the reception, despite his nagging, I caught Jeff loading up on goodies from the fountain when he thought no one else was looking!)

Sure, I ended up paying for more than I anticipated, but it was so worth it! I also completely understand why people elope. Thankfully, every time I began to panic, like all great wedding planners, Chad talked me off the ledge.

Chad became like family to Jonathan and me. As for Jeff? Well, he and Chad didn't really see eye to eye. Maybe Jeff was worried that I suddenly had a new gay bestie. I would have enjoyed Jeff getting to know Jonathan's family and helping with the seating chart and other details. I understand that he has a really full life, but this was my wedding and in my mind, I had really hoped that he'd want to do those things with me. But the reality remains, it's not really who Jeff is. My expectation was unfair to place on him because he couldn't live up to it. I couldn't get upset over it.

What's the point?

It got me thinking, though. It might be fun to renew my vows every year just to annoy Jeff.

Once I had picked out the design it was time to figure out the music—and I had wanted both a DJ and a band for our wedding. While Jeff was with me in Chicago, he and I were scheduled to appear on the last episode of the *Rosie O'Donnell Show* in March 2012. While we were backstage, one of her producers introduced me to Parker Williams, the DJ for her show, suggesting that he might be a great DJ for my wedding.

We got to talking and just connected about old-school hip-hop, which he had grown up with and loved as much as I do. I told him about the kids' rap album I was working on, thinking he might be perfect to help with some beats. And, coincidentally, Parker also happened to live five floors above Jonathan in the same building, so I guess it was meant to be. Parker said he'd love to DJ the wedding. After going through several producers and beat artists while recording my album, I knew Parker was the answer to my prayers to get my project done. To test the collaborative process together, I suggested that we work on a rap song as a thank-you gift to all of our friends and family attending the wedding, as well as a rap for Jonathan that I could surprise him with at the reception. Parker rolled with all of my ideas and became my go-to guy for everything music.

Once we got all of the details of the reception in order, I tortured Jonathan with the tedious process of registering for wedding gifts. It was St. Patrick's Day in Chicago, a near religious experience for the great people of that city, and where were Jonathan and I?

Bloomingdales'!

I took a picture of Jonathan staring out the window of the store, looking like he was in detention at school while all of his friends were outside playing in the yard.

"Jon, do you want these salt and pepper shakers or those?

"How about this platter?

"How many glasses should we get?"

He'd mumble his response while holding the scanning gun to the item he preferred.

Beep.

"Got it!" he'd say.

At one point, we looked over and noticed another guy in the store who had clearly been there for a while, too. We actually took a lunch break, came back, and he was still there. When I commented on his amazing attitude, the guy turned to us and said with a straight face, "I'm suicidal."

Thankfully, Jonathan is a patient man. Hours in an operating room will teach you to stay focused and get through anything—even registering for china at Bloomingdale's.

I think every woman deserves to feel like a princess on her wedding day if she wants to. After all, it's her day and the one single time you can selfishly indulge your every wish without guilt or remorse. For me, that meant walking down the aisle in the most beautiful gown I could imagine. I was so honored that Marc Bouwer agreed to create my wedding gown. He is such a wonderfully talented designer whose work I truly admire. He was my first and only choice, and boy, did I make the right decision!

I wanted a dress with long sleeves because, um, well, I am a little older than the average bride—still a hot fox, but well, okay, I'll say it again, *older*. The lace that Marc picked was stunning. The back of the dress plunged to the base of my spine, while the front had a strapless look. From the waist down, the gown was full and flowed perfectly. I chose a long train because it felt so regal to me. I was inspired by Kate Middleton's train, and thought it would be beautiful coming down the aisle of our Greek church. Jonathan's niece was our flower girl, so Marc made her a matching dress from the very same lace. It also had the same train as mine. For us, that represented two families joining together.

When I put on my gown the day of my wedding, I felt so peaceful. It was ironic because everything around me felt crazy and yet I was able to take a step back for ten minutes or so, breathe, and just say, "Wow."

Jonathan and I had gone to the church early that morning to have a private moment before the big event. Something bigger I believed took over from that point on. I felt genuine serenity—perhaps for the first time in my life. I liked the way it felt.

As I made my way down the aisle later that day, I could feel all of the warmth and love emanating in the church, es-

*Walking on air in
Jonathan's
Windy City.
(Photo Credit:
Rick Aguilar)*

pecially as I drew closer to Jonathan, looking dashing in his tuxedo. I could barely fight back the tears of joy that were filling my eyes. There was so much to celebrate that day—my sister, who was my matron of honor, had been cancer-free for a year and a half. Everywhere I looked, I saw a miracle.

Sometime during the weekend, and before the ceremony, my mom and dad unexpectedly came to a resolution in their relationship—another miracle, because after years, she finally had closure. My mom, dad, and his wife rode in a limousine together to the church. That was an unthinkable scenario until my wedding day. I was truly overwhelmed by my parents' decision to put aside their differences and make it a true celebration of love.

When you put a lot of work into something, you *can* get a great result. Our reception was insanely fun and over-the-top gorgeous. Although I had spent months planning for this moment, I hadn't seen the room in its entirety until I walked through the door as Mrs. Nassos. When we walked into the room, Tommy Shaw, from the band Styx was there to sing to us. Jonathan and I had seen Styx perform at the Greek Theater in Hollywood a month earlier and loved it! Tommy and Jeannie are clients of Jeff's, so imagine my surprise when *he* arranged to have him sing at our wedding. He also took my mom into the ballroom to show it to her in advance, like a

At my wedding with my TV better half, Jeff Lewis.

proud brother. Turns out, Jeff did care about my wedding and this was his way of showing it.

Tommy wrote a song for his wife Jeanie called "Yes I Can" that meant a lot to both of them, which he performed for us that night. Everyone loved it, especially Jonathan and I. During our ceremony, the priest talked about our relationship being a rose that needs to be cultivated. He said it would have thorns, but if you water it and take care of it, it will grow. When Tommy sang the words, "I can see you in the garden tending your roses . . ." it was another miracle I didn't see coming. It was a moment for all of us—even Tommy, who shared with the crowd that he felt so nervous that night, even after thirty years of performing. Tommy's performance will be one of those memories I will replay over and over in my mind for the rest of my life.

When it came to love, I was now on a steep learning curve, blissfully happy and so deeply grateful that I finally found what I was looking for. Looking back at my early life, I have no regrets about not becoming a doctor. After all, I ended up marrying one! If you trust the process, things do have a way of working out.

My father's speech that night was lovely. He spoke about what a wonderful job my mom did as a parent to their children and how grateful he was to her because she had always remained a loving wife, mother, and friend. With these affirming and sincere words, I could visibly see a weight lifted from my mother's shoulders that she had been carrying around since the day my dad left us. I hadn't expected this to happen, but I am grateful and thankful that it did.

I can also say that today my father and I are in a great place, even if I don't agree with all of his decisions. I am grateful that he gave me a lot of my crazy and creative traits. He is such a forward-thinking man, something I am proud to say he has passed on to me. We now have a relationship that we are both happy to share.

As I took in every moment of that very special day, my prayers had been answered. I had finally embraced the true meaning of guidance, wisdom, family, and home. For us, and for our families, this was a happy new beginning.

14

And Baby Makes Three

> You know you're in love when you can't fall asleep
> because reality is finally better than your dreams.
>
> —DR. SEUSS

Once the dust settled from our incredible wedding weekend, Jonathan and I had to face that it was time for him to
leave his family and friends in Chicago and move back to Los
Angeles to live with me as husband and wife. When we met,
I was only working on *Flipping Out*. By the time we married,
I'd added a new show, *Interior Therapy with Jeff Lewis*.. The
premise of the show involves us spending a week with clients
to do a total life renovation from cleaning up their homes to
their relationships and everything in between. The humor is
not lost on me that we ended up with a show about helping
others work out their relationships when ours was so deeply
rooted in dysfunction. I don't regret a single moment that has

led me to where I am today, because in the end, so much good has come from the success of *Flipping Out* and now, *Interior Therapy with Jeff Lewis*.

These days, there's a clear difference in what it feels like for Jeff and for me, now that I am fully present and engaged in our work together. Jeff can see that I have respected my work with him and given it the attention it requires. I find that I am more creative and therefore a better asset to his business. I am here and excited about design.

And when it comes to acting, the impact of being fully engaged has allowed me a lot more freedom and even though it's scarier, it's a lot more fun. I used to get flustered by getting a line wrong or blowing a take. These days I just do it again until I nail it!

And last, but certainly not least, being present in my personal relationships has brought me the one thing I never thought I'd have again—true love with a man who is far too good for a needy, crazy girl like me!

I was honest with Jonathan from the start about wanting to be in Los Angeles for work. Relocating could have been the end of my career and I wasn't ready to quit what I'd worked so hard to achieve. Jonathan could practice medicine in California, but I couldn't continue working at my present momentum if I moved to Chicago. Every time I mentioned I wouldn't move to Chicago, he let me know he was clear on that decision and supported it.

Jonathan is a lot better at embracing the unknown than I

am. His training as a physician requires him to handle high-stress situations in a calm and rational manner. He is capable of being patient and knows how to be willing to stay the course. These are not traits I've been well known for.

I'd moved around from Oregon to Arizona when I was a kid, and then to California for college. I hadn't lived in any one place my entire life so I didn't have the same kind of tie to a city like Jonathan has to Chicago. Aside from the year he spent in L.A. doing his fellowship, Jonathan had been in Chicago for thirty-four years. I understood the sacrifice Jonathan was making and wanted to be as supportive as I could throughout the packing, the move, and his early weeks in L.A. Although he wasn't showing it, I think Jonathan was terrified about starting over. He'd built a very nice practice in Chicago and would be faced with starting from square one. He told me that if he really didn't believe that my career could make a difference in people's lives in a positive way, he would have asked me to pack it in and come to Chicago. But he didn't. He truly believes in me and my dreams. As a result, he was giving up everything, including his friends and proximity to his family. Jonathan comes from a very close-knit group of Greeks, and though they were supportive of his decision, it was hard to let him go. I understand that feeling because I didn't want to be without him either.

Jonathan moved to Los Angeles in September 2012 with the difficult task of rebuilding his life and career from the ground up. He courageously began in a new city, making new contacts and building new friendships. His life was now exposed because his wife is on a reality television show, but he still had chosen to leave Chicago for us.

What was he thinking?

We started our life together in Los Angeles, learning to connect even deeper by finally being together in one place long enough to bond as husband and wife. This kind of togetherness definitely has its perks!

Shortly after we settled in to married life, we unexpectedly discovered that I was pregnant. We had talked about wanting to start a family, but we weren't exactly *trying*.

Practicing—often—but not trying to get pregnant!

My fortieth birthday was just around the corner so there was some concern that I might have a hard time conceiving because of my age. Jonathan was open to whatever we needed to do, whether it was IVF treatments or adoption, so long as we did our best to start a family together.

Lots of people were rooting for us to get in the game right away. Jeff's grandmother's advice was my favorite: "Just have a couple of glasses of wine, relax, and *enjoy!*" She also told me that if I really wanted to get knocked up, I should tuck my knees into my chest after having sex.

Confused and not wanting to sound creepy I asked her, "Is it knees forward or back?"

"It's knees forward and chest up!" she said with great gusto!

Suspecting something was different and being unusually late, I took a home pregnancy test. When I showed the results to Jonathan, he was speechless.

At the time, we had been planning a getaway to Hawaii before I had to start filming the second season of *Interior Therapy with Jeff Lewis*. My gynecologist said she was concerned that I would miscarry because my hormone levels were very low and dropping, which indicates a possible weak pregnancy. She strongly advised us to cancel our trip.

I was very upset and torn by my doctor's warning. I called my former gynecologist for a second opinion. I had stopped seeing her because she was no longer delivering babies. I was sobbing on the phone as I explained my situation.

"Jenni, women are walking with jugs on their heads in Africa while carrying babies. If you are going to maintain this pregnancy, you will, and your baby will be fine. Go on your trip," she said.

Jonathan and I really needed to get away. I wanted some uninterrupted quality time with my husband before the craziness of my shooting schedule interfered with my life and before Jonathan got busy with his work. We had taken a short trip to Cabo San Lucas, Mexico, as a honeymoon after the wedding, but because of professional obligations, it was a very short trip. After weighing the pros and cons, we still thought that this trip to Hawaii was a much-needed respite.

Nature has a way of taking care of itself, especially when it comes to pregnancies that just aren't meant to be. Sadly, I suffered a miscarriage in Hawaii. I felt very peaceful about it, yet emotional for our loss. At the same time, I was extremely grateful to know that I could get pregnant.

Unaware that I had been pregnant or that I had just

miscarried, my dearest friend Kami called me while we were in Hawaii. She said she'd had a crazy dream that I was going to have a baby. She told me that she saw the ocean and a little girl standing there waiting and wanting to come to us. Although I didn't tell her what had just happened, I was very moved by her call, and hoped with every ounce of my being that she was right.

When we got back to Los Angeles, Jonathan and I decided to try again right away. I went to the doctor to get some definitive answers on when we could start to try again. She saw something on the sonogram that looked a little confusing and suggested we do a blood test to see what was going on.

I left her office and went straight to shoot an episode of the second season of *Interior Therapy with Jeff Lewis* at the home of two men who were our clients for the week.

We were having dinner when one of the guys turned to me and said, "You are pregnant!"

"No . . ." I said.

"Yes, you are." He was insistent.

He walked around the dining room table and began touching my tummy. "I can always tell, and you, my dear, are definitely pregnant!"

Okay, this was a little weird. I explained that I had just had a miscarriage and that perhaps he was picking up on that. I denied the notion as even being possible.

When I left their house that night, I checked my telephone messages from the car. There was a missed call from my doctor.

"Honey, it's kind of spooky, but I did your blood test and you are pregnant again! Your hormone levels are very high this time, making me very optimistic that this will be a viable pregnancy. Congratulations!" She was genuinely happy and thrilled for me.

When I got home, I played the message for Jonathan.

He was speechless . . . again. He could hardly believe what he was hearing.

Neither could I.

My mind reeled with thoughts on whether I'd be a good mother, was the timing of this right, could I do this? I get overwhelmed so easily. Was I really ready for this? The truth is, there really is no perfect time for anything that changes your life forever. You just do it and then figure it out.

A friend of mine said, "All a baby really needs in the beginning is you, a bottle, and a blanket."

Something about those words calmed my mind.

Jonathan had been through so much change in the months since he left Chicago. He handled it all with beautiful grace.

And me?

Being pregnant has been my greatest lesson in embracing the unknown and being at peace with it. I don't know what to expect and probably never will, but this time around, I am fully committed to doing the work, to put the baby's needs before my own, and learn to be the very best mom I can be. I have finally let go of my need to prove to the world I am someone—that I matter. There's something and someone in my life that is so much bigger than me now.

Alianna made us a family—2013. (Lori Dorman photography)

Dear Baby Alianna,

You have immediately made my life a happier place to be, and we just met! I stare at you and see innocence, determination, and strength. Stay that way, my baby girl. I hope I can teach you how to embrace failure and to not be afraid.

Your father loves you so much. You should see the way he looks at you. I know how much he loves me when I see how much he loves you. I want this for you someday.

He loves when you have a poopy diaper, too! That will be embarrassing one day, sorry! You make us both so very proud.

There was a time I was down and thought someone like you would never come into my life. That God didn't want that for me. I had to Grin and Bear It. I'm so glad I did.

You were waiting for the right time, and let me tell you, you were *so* worth the wait.

If everyone out there doesn't believe good things are waiting for them, they are wrong. It just wasn't about my timing. It was about yours.

The world is ahead of you and it is so exciting. Please remember to try not to go "juvenile delinquent" on me.

I will be here for you every day of my life.

Baby, it's all about *you*, now, and I couldn't be happier about that.

xoxo

Mom

MY MOM'S WORRY LIST

I worry my daughter will become a juvenile delinquent. Check

I worry my daughter will get divorced or marry the wrong man. Check

I worry my daughter will embarrass me. Check

I worry my daughter will end up "on the cutting-room floor." Check

I worry that she will eat and drink too much. Check

I worry she will make me cook for her when I am old.
Check

I worry she will have more than one big wedding. Check

I worry she will never be okay and never be happy. NO
CHECK

See Mom? It all worked out.

Acknowledgments

God, you answered my prayers when you were ready and I am sorry for not being understanding of that in the moment. You have given me the desires of my heart and I love you with all that I am. Thank you for not strangling me.

Mom, aka Alice, you are my inspiration. You have lived your life with dignity, obedience, faith, and love. Yes, I tease you about your negativity and lack of nurturing, but I know you did the absolute best you could, which is all any of us can do. My prayer is that I can be for Alianna everything wonderful I now realize you have been for me. I promise I will call you every day when you are ninety-three with the latest "juvenile delinquent" updates.

Dad, I love you and thank you for being the best dad you could be. Because I am your daughter I have been blessed with many gifts. I appreciate every wonderful thing about you. You can always make 'em laugh. Thanks for all you did for me.

Krisann, my beautiful sister, you are my best pal and hero. The love letter you wrote to cancer was more proof of your faith, strength, grace, beauty, and determination. Take a bow, celebrate your many talents, and embrace that many more dreams will come true in your life.

To the men of the Kontaxis Family—Dr. Euthym, Michael, Nicholas, and Christian—your faith is an inspiration, and your humor often smoothed my bumpy road. Dr. Euthym, you have been a rock star. Nicholas, pray for me. Michael, cast me in your movies. Christian, can you operate on me when I am old?

Jonathan Nassos, you are my best friend, partner in faith, and the love of my life. You were worth the wait. You are more than what I prayed for, wished for, and dreamed about. Thank you for every day. If life was taken from me tomorrow I have experienced true love and a peace with you that I could never have imagined. You have made my mom so happy. I wish love like this for everyone out there. Even on the days I want to shoot you.

To the Nassos Family, you have given me a man who gave my life meaning. I will always treasure your faith, love, and support. You have very powerful genes. Alianna looks just like Jonathan.

To Lulu, Janet, and Alianna, my three favorite girls in the whole world. My heart is always with you. You are my every-things. The three of you are tremendous supporters of the arts. I thank you for your endless love and for calling me Mom.

To Father James Tavlarides, I'm thanking God for you.

To Dr. Ron Kvitne, his lovely wife Kal, and their beautiful daughter, Aliki, thank you for introducing me to my husband.

To Jeff Lewis: We have had a wild ride and I love you no matter what life brings our way. You are passionate, extremely talented, and have a big heart. Yes, I have wanted to kill you, and probably always will, but don't worry it will never happen.

My mazel of the day goes to Andy Cohen, my loyal friend with the 411. Your friendship has been a huge gift and I so admire your willingness to "go toward the hit" in your own life. You are full of chutzpah, talent, and warmth.

To all my friends at Bravo: God bless each and every one of you for allowing me to be SEEN.

To Jeff Lewis Design, for putting up with "Mom."

To Chaz Dean: Your genius gave me long beautiful hair. I am grateful for such a kind, dear friend. My hair was gorgeous on my wedding day because you did it.

To all the teachers, bosses, coworkers, and Hollywood experts who told me I was a nonstop failure, that I couldn't do it, and rewarded my bad behavior: A better-late-than-never thank-you. With your help I have become less self-involved, more confident, and the barely famous woman I am today.

To the St. Martin's Team: Kathy Huck and John Murphy, who, after their experience with this curly-haired girl, may want to go into early retirement. Thank you for championing me. Thanks, also, to Jeanne-Marie Hudson, John Karle, Kim Ludlam, Kate Ottaviano, Nancy Trypuc, and the rest of the gang.

To Authentic Entertainment, you were my first big showbiz "Yes." I am forever grateful.

To Chris Elwood: I know you have a new life; I wish you the best always.

To Laura Morton: Thanks for sharing your expertise with Kathleen and me on this long journey. You have no idea what it meant that a talented bestselling author was interested in